SURVIVAL!
AT SEA

Other Books in the
SURVIVAL! *Series*
from Avon Camelot

SURVIVAL! IN THE MOUNTAINS
by Ken McMurtry

Coming Soon

SURVIVAL! IN THE JUNGLE
by Susan Landsman

SURVIVAL! IN THE DESERT
by Susan Landsman

SUSAN LANDSMAN is the author of two other books for Avon Camelot, *What Happened to Amelia Earhart* and *Who Shot JFK?*

She lives in Hinesburg, Vermont, with her husband and two children.

SURVIVAL! AT SEA

SUSAN LANDSMAN

Illustrated by Rose Water

AN AVON CAMELOT BOOK

SURVIVAL! AT SEA is an original publication of Avon Books. This work has never before appeared in book form.

AVON BOOKS
A division of
The Hearst Corporation
1350 Avenue of the Americas
New York, New York 10019

Copyright © 1993 by Whitbread Books
Cover photo courtesy of Tony Stone Worldwide
Published by arrangement with Whitbread Books
Library of Congress Catalog Card Number: 92-31929
ISBN: 0-380-76603-5
RL: 5.6

Library of Congress Cataloging in Publication Data:
Landsman, Susan.
    Survival! at sea / by Susan Landsman.
        p.   cm.
Includes bibliographical references.
1. Survival after airplane accidents, shipwrecks, etc.   I. Title.
G525.L353   1993
910.4'5—dc20

92-31929
CIP AC

First Avon Camelot Printing: March 1993

CAMELOT TRADEMARK REG. U.S. PAT. OFF. AND IN OTHER COUNTRIES, MARCA REGISTRADA, HECHO EN U.S.A.

Printed in the U.S.A.

OPM   10   9   8   7   6   5   4   3   2   1

Contents

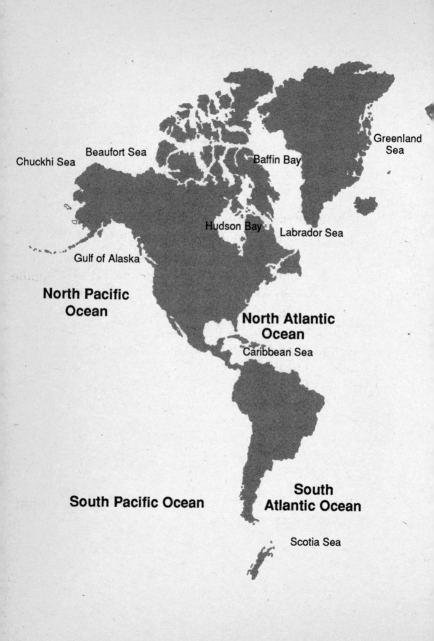

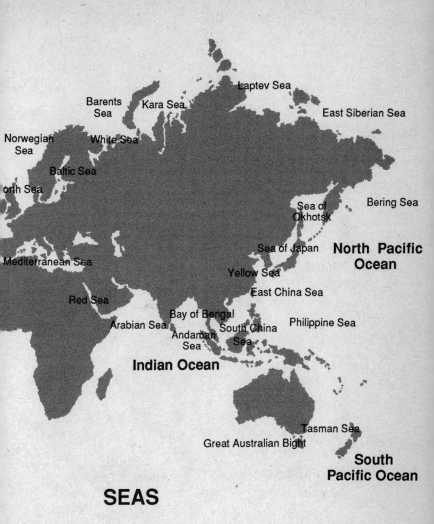

SEAS

Chapter 1

Shipwrecked!

Maralyn and Maurice Bailey were a typical English couple. She was a tax officer, he a printer's clerk. They each spent five days a week working at their jobs, but in the evenings they built their dreams. The Baileys longed to leave England and sail toward a new life in New Zealand. For years, Maralyn and Maurice saved their money to buy the ship of their dreams. The thirty-one-foot sailing sloop was custom built. She could steer easily and had full headroom below deck. Maurice and Maralyn named her the *Auralyn,* a combination of their two names.

The English couple set sail from Panama on February 27, 1973. They were bound for the Galapagos Islands, a ten-day sail on the Pacific Ocean. The weather was perfect for days—clear skies, light winds, and a calm sea. But on March 4, their sixth day at sea, disaster struck. A trip that should have lasted less than two weeks, turned into a 117-day attempt to survive at sea.

March 4: Bam! A forty-foot sperm whale rams the *Auralyn*. There's a hole about eighteen inches long and twelve inches wide in the boat below the water-line. Maralyn and Maurice try desperately to pump out the water that's rushing in. They push a blanket into the hole hoping to plug it, but in moments the blanket is soaked through. After forty minutes of attempting to save it, the shocked couple abandon ship. They gather some food and gear and board their life raft. They load the supplies into their dinghy which is tied to the raft. Then Maralyn and Maurice Bailey watch their dreams disappear under the sea. Not a trace of the *Auralyn* remains.

After taking inventory, they see that they have enough food and water to last twenty days if they ration it. Surely they'll be rescued by then. After all, they're close to a shipping route so they're bound to be picked up soon. The first night in the raft they take turns every three hours keeping watch for passing ships.

March 5: The next morning Maurice checks the water supply. Four gallons of their water have been contaminated by seawater! Now it's unfit to drink. Maralyn rigs a sail hoping to increase their drifting speed. She uses two oars as masts and the sail bag as her sail. It's a good sail, but there's no wind. They begin to bake in the hot sun on the open sea. They soak their spare clothes in seawater. They drape the cool, wet garments on their bodies to get the cooling effect of the water evaporating.

Prehistoric-looking turtles swim up to the raft.

Maralyn is worried that they'll chafe the raft and cause a rip. She hits them over the head with a paddle. The turtles swim away but are back ten minutes later when their headaches are gone.

March 12: Maralyn decides to capture a turtle alive. She grabs one by the flippers, and although it is very heavy, she hurls it into the dinghy thinking maybe they can kill it and use it as fish bait.

Suddenly she spots a ship! They pull a flare from their emergency kit, but it's a dud. They pull out another and wave the orange light. They use two more. Still there's no response from the ship. With the last flare, the Baileys watch the ship move away. Why weren't they seen? It's early morning. Maralyn thinks the ship must be on automatic pilot. The crew is probably down below eating breakfast.

She returns to the turtle in the dinghy. Yes, he'll make good bait. But when she looks for the fishing line and hooks, Maralyn realizes that they forgot to repack them into the emergency kit when they left Panama. Their fishing equipment went down with the *Auralyn*. Now the turtle will be food instead of bait.

March 13: Maralyn and Maurice agree on a plan for killing the turtle. Maurice will hit it over the head with a paddle to immobilize it. Then Maralyn will slit its throat. It's a struggle to take the turtle's life. The skin is leathery and hard to cut. It saddens them both to do it. When it's finally cut, a lot of blood pours over the side of the boat. All kinds of fish show up immediately to drink the blood. Maralyn can barely wash her hands in the sea without being nipped by a fish.

They cut the turtle into large steaks and throw the carcass overboard. Maralyn is still determined to fish. She takes a safety pin from their first aid kit and cuts it in two with pliers. She bends the pin into a hook and threads cord for fishing line through the bottom spring hoop of the pin. Now Maralyn has fishing gear, but the turtle meat is too soft for bait. The fish just pull it off and swim away. The turtle's membranes are tougher. With membrane bait, Maralyn catches several triggerfish. She pulls them into the dinghy and hits them on the head until they're dead.

Maralyn grabs the slippery triggerfish and hits it on the back of its head with a mariner's knife until it is dead. Whenever they eat triggerfish, Maurice guts the fish and Maralyn cuts off the heads. Next, Maurice slits the underside and Maralyn cuts the flesh away from the backbone. Finally, Maurice strips the fillets out. They eat the white meat raw and also the eyeballs, which have been cut out of the head. The eyeballs are filled with a thirst-quenching liquid.

Triggerfish become the Baileys' main diet. They're easy to catch, fillet, and eat raw or dried. Catching them does leave battle scars, though. The fish bite and their spines make cuts in both their hands that get infected.

March 21: The inside of the raft is getting wet from sea spray. Maurice and Maralyn spend a lot of time mopping the raft with sponges. Their lower bodies are chafed all over from so much contact with the rubber surface of the raft. Blisters are forming everywhere.

It begins to rain and the heat subsides. The Baileys rig up a system to catch rainwater. The water drips down the canopy (the roof of the raft) and runs through the air vent chute. They set a bucket under the vent to collect the water. This rain can't be wasted, so they also mop up water from the floor of the raft. They squeeze it into containers and taste it. The water is contaminated by the chemicals in the waterproof coating on the raft. But after an hour, a lot of the coating is washed off and they collect a pint of drinkable water. That's a full day's ration for one person.

They catch and kill a second turtle. Surprisingly, the fat beneath the shell is tasty. They mop up more water. The work to survive is continual. Both Maurice and Maralyn are becoming tired and so thin that their ribs show through their skin.

March 29: At 3:45 a.m., Maralyn spots another ship! She quickly grabs a flare, but again, it's a dud. The next, and last, flare works well. The area all around the raft is lit up. Maurice flashes an SOS with his flashlight. But the ship sails out of sight.

April 8: The Baileys have been adrift for over a month. Their progress toward the Galapagos is slow. Maurice hitches some ropes tied to the raft onto a sea turtle. He catches the turtle, puts the rope around its flippers, and sets it back in the sea. Sure enough, the turtle heads in the right direction. Hoping for two turtlepower, Maurice hooks up to another turtle. But this guy is headed in the opposite direction. Maurice unties him, pulling a suckerfish from the turtle's belly to use as fish bait.

April 10: At 10:00 a.m. another ship! There are no more flares left, but the couple wave their oilskins furiously. The ship remains on its course and disappears among the waves. The next time a ship passes, the Baileys will be better prepared. They decide to make their own flares.

When they abandoned the *Auralyn,* Maralyn had grabbed some clothes on hangers. Now she removes the hanger hook and ties strips of cloth around the rest of it. Her idea is to soak the cloth-covered hangers in kerosene and methylated spirits so they'll ignite quickly.

Maralyn also makes a smoke flare from a cake tin. She tears pages from a book and rolls the paper into tight screws. The paper screws and cloth scraps are placed in the tin. The next time a ship passes, she'll light the tin contents and then use the cover to damper the fire down and emit smoke.

April 12: At 3:30 p.m. Maralyn hears a ship. She grabs her tin smoke flare and places it inside a turtle shell for safety. She ignites the paper and cloth. It makes big flames but not much smoke. Maralyn rushes for a wet towel to dampen the flames. She holds the tin high and the smoke billows out.

Suddenly, the ship stops. It begins to turn. It's moving away! But wait—it turns again 180 degrees.

Is it coming toward them? The Baileys watch, scarcely breathing, and then the ship turns 180 degrees again and sails away. What happened? Most likely, the ship saw the Baileys for a moment. But when the crew looked again, the raft had disappeared in the waves. The weather is getting rougher. Maurice prays that the water will calm before another ship passes. It's difficult to be seen in these swells.

April 18: Still another ship passes. They can't light the homemade flare because water got mixed in with the kerosene, and the matches are all damp.

Maralyn and Maurice have been keeping one of the turtles as a pet for the last two weeks. He's about two feet long and named Rastus. Rastus has been living in the dinghy with wet rags on him. They lower him into the water twice a day for a swim.

April 20: Rastus is dead. They were fond of their pet, but he was also their reserve food supply. Now they'll butcher and eat him. The Baileys eat breakfast slowly, clean up, and then doze on and off until evening. Evening is the best time to fish. They read, play word games, and talk about life before and after the accident. Even though they've been adrift for forty-seven days and five ships have passed them by, they make plans to build a new yacht once they're saved. They draw an outline for building their new boat. In fact, this becomes their favorite topic.

April 24: Today is Maralyn's birthday so Maurice wants to catch a silver milkfish as a special treat.

But these are big fish, and the hook isn't strong enough to hold one. As the fish breaks free, the hook springs back into the dinghy. Maurice yanks it out and air hisses in his face. The dinghy has a leak!

Maurice follows the instructions on the repair kit: he dries and cleans the leaking area, applies the glue, and then patiently holds the dinghy out of the water until the glue dries. The patch seems to work, but a container with a four-day supply of water was lost in the mishap.

April 26: The dinghy patch has floated away. The glue plugs the hole a little, but the craft has to be pumped up at least twice a day.

April 28: Now the raft is punctured. There's a row of tiny holes made by the back of a spinefoot fish. Spinefoot fish rest under the raft for shade. One was probably startled by a predator so it rose its spines in defense. The result? A neat row of holes on the raft floor.

Patching doesn't work. Desperately, Maralyn and Maurice pump the raft every fifteen to twenty minutes to keep the floor firm. At night they pump every thirty to forty minutes. Sometimes they both fall asleep and wake up trapped in folds of rubber.

Early May: The days flow together. The water in containers in the dinghy is contaminated. Sun baking on the polyethylene containers turned the water green. Only the water in jugs in the raft is drinkable since it's protected from the sun under the canopy. The Baileys continue to eat turtle and drink rainwater. They live exhausted, in despair.

May 8: The sixth ship passes. The Baileys think they can make it for two more weeks. Maurice has a hacking cough. They are both so cold and wet that they probably have pneumonia.

May 18: The seventh ship comes and goes. It has been raining for weeks, so when the sun finally shines, the Baileys feel released from the agonizing wetness. Maurice's body is cold yet he's feverish. He can't lift his arms because he's in so much pain. His hacking cough keeps them both awake, and sometimes he coughs up blood. Maralyn catches their twenty-second turtle. It's a female and has 150–200 eggs inside. They're a delicacy and give Maurice some energy.

Late in the day sharks hit the bottom of the raft. They butt at it. They don't harm the raft, but each time a shark hits, Maurice and Maralyn cry out because their buttocks have too little flesh over the bones to absorb the pain.

May 31: It's the eighty-eighth day adrift. The Baileys have tried to maintain good hygiene to reduce the risk of infections. They use an empty biscuit tin in the dinghy as a toilet. They wash their hair and clean their teeth in seawater. It's too cold to bathe in the rain.

June 5: This is the worst day so far. Because it's stormy, they have to bale out the raft all night. It's *so* cold. As the waves toss the craft about, the raft and dinghy don't always ride the wave together. They get out of phase.

9

With great force, a huge wave breaks over the raft. The dinghy overturns with Maurice in it. Luckily, Maralyn is in the raft—she doesn't know how to swim! Maralyn waits anxiously for Maurice to surface. In a few minutes, though it seems like hours, Maurice comes up. He struggles to turn the dinghy back up. The wind is against him and he is weak. With every last ounce of strength, Maurice finally turns the dinghy up, but their bait and fishing gear are gone.

The Baileys prepare for another capsize. They put their canned food, knives, and can opener into a sack and lash the sack to the raft. If the dinghy or raft go over, at least the supplies will stay with it. It has been storming for four days. There are no fish to catch since they will wait out the storm in the calmer, deeper layers of the sea.

June 6: Finally, the storm subsides. Maralyn catches a turtle and they heave it into the dinghy.

June 10: A seabird called the blue-footed booby keeps landing on their craft. Maralyn is concerned that the bird's excrements will contaminate their food and water. She hits the bird with a paddle to discourage it from staying. It throws up four, whole flying fish. That was an easy catch!

June 12: One hundred days in the raft have passed. It occurs to the Baileys that the seabirds may be edible. This time when a booby lands, Maralyn wraps a towel around her hand and grabs it by the feet. They kill the bird, pluck it, and eat it raw. It's a nice change from all the fish they've been eating. Some days they catch over a hundred triggerfish.

June 21: Sharks are bumping and circling the raft. Without thinking, Maralyn grabs one by the tail! She shouts for Maurice who is ready with a towel. Maralyn flips the shark into the raft and Maurice holds its biting end. After a fifteen minute struggle the shark is dead.

Maralyn is energized by her conquest. She catches three more sharks. Maurice begs her to stop because there's no more room in the dinghy! Boobies continue to come right to the raft. Needless to say, the Baileys now have plenty to eat. Maurice is feeling better.

For the next few days, larger sharks buffet the raft. When the impact hits Maurice's sores, they open and bleed. One shark attack lasts for over a half hour. They seem to always hit the raft, not the dinghy, even if the Baileys are in the dinghy. Maurice and Maralyn wonder if it is the color they see underwater that attracts them. The raft is black and the dinghy is gray.

Late June: Maralyn has a brainstorm for catching fish that will require little energy. Energy is one commodity the Baileys are fast running out of. She takes the one-gallon container leftover from the kerosene. It's blue plastic with a handle on top and a spout on one end. She takes off the cap and threads live bait into the container. Then she lowers the container into the water by the handle.

This idea takes patience and ingenuity. First, Maralyn will "train" the fish. Fish swim into the

Sharks

The good news about sharks is that they don't live in swimming pools, rivers, ponds, or lakes. In fact, *most* sharks are found in tropical and temperate seas where the water is over seventy degrees. Almost all human attacks have happened in warm water. True, not many people swim in cold ocean water. But research also shows that a shark's appetite is affected by water temperature. The warmer the water, the hungrier they are.

It's *not* true that every shark will attack. While one moves in for the kill, another will simply circle around and swim away. Sharks have been known to pick out just one person in a crowd of swimmers and attack him only. No one knows why for certain (see *Sharks Do's and Don'ts* for some possibilities). We just don't know what's going on in the shark's brain. But we do know that their brains are tiny. Even the largest of sharks has only a three-inch brain.

What they do have is a great sense of smell. They can detect blood hundreds of yards away. Once they sniff their prey, these creatures give new meaning to the word dangerous. Their bodies are covered with sharp *placoid scales.* Just a slap of a shark's tail can cut through a rubber raft or a swimmer's skin.

These deadly creatures are most famous for their jaws. They have several sets of needle-sharp teeth that function as spare tires. The teeth are set loosely in the jaw. If one tooth gets broken off, the "spare" just moves right into place. A shark bite is very deep. It hits the arteries. Victims usually die from blood loss before they get to shore.

Sharks will eat just about anything. A shark captured in Australia had half a ham, the hindquarters of a pig, the head and front legs of a bulldog with a rope around its neck, and several legs of mutton inside. Another captured in the Adriatic Sea preferred a different type of cuisine entirely. It contained three overcoats, a nylon raincoat, and a car license plate.

Actually, not all sharks are killers. Of the 250 species of shark, only about twelve species are threatening. These include the great white shark, the mako shark, the hammerhead, requiem, tiger, and lemon sharks. (See pictures.)

We tend to think of the shark's fin as an evil sign. But it's easily confused with other fish. A shark's fin sticks just above the surface of the water. A porpoise also has a fin above water, but it also shows some of its back. The swordfish reveals some of its tail when it swims, and this resembles a shark fin. The manta ray shows two parallel wing tips that also look like the dreaded fin.

trap to feed and she lets them. They can feast and leave. This way, they learn not to fear the trap and will swim into it readily. Maralyn catches twenty triggerfish for breakfast the next morning with little bait, less effort, and no chance of losing their fishhook.

June 30: The Baileys have enough to eat, but they're weak and tired. They are lucky if they sleep an hour at a stretch. It's so hot, they feel they will wither away.

Maurice drifts off into a restless sleep. Maralyn looks dreamily toward the horizon. Suddenly she sits upright and leans into the wind. "Maurice! Maurice!" she cries. "Wake up, I hear a ship!" It has been forty-three days since the last ship passed. This is ship number eight. Will this be the one that finally notices the emaciated couple after 117 days adrift at sea?

The Baileys *do* survive their harrowing ordeal. Their story tells us a lot about the will to live and the ability of human beings to adapt and improvise in difficult situations. When you imagine yourself in Maralyn or Maurice's place, do you think you could make it? No?

Well, think again and read on. By the time you finish reading this book, you may change your mind. You'll learn a lot about the wonders of the sea. You'll also learn the facts about boating, because you can't be safe unless you know what you're getting yourself into. And yes, you will find out what finally happened to the Baileys.

The various types of shark you might encounter on the open seas.

Shark Do's and Don'ts

On a Boat

- Don't tow speared fish in the water. That's like inviting a shark for supper. Put them in your boat immediately.

- Wash out blood-soaked sponges from cleaning fish. Throw the fish head and bones as far as you can. Sharks can detect one part blood per *million* parts water. That's like smelling out one particular steak dinner out of every dinner plate in Boston.

- Don't trail your arms or legs from the life raft.

- Carry an object at least three feet long on your boat to prod sharks away.

In the Water

- Don't swim alone or where sharks have been sighted.

- Don't go in the water if you have a bleeding wound.

- Take off jewelry before you swim. Flashing objects attract sharks.

- Don't wear contrasting colors like a white swimsuit against a deep tan or black skin. It's easier for the sharks to see.

- Don't swim at night or in murky water during the day. That's shark turf.

- If you spot a shark while swimming, try not to panic. Swim away smoothly and get out of the water as quickly as possible. Thrashing in the water will invite the shark to you.

- If you see a shark and can't get out of the water, stay calm and *keep looking at the shark*. They rarely attack people facing them.

- If a shark seems ready to attack, scream at it. Some divers have frightened sharks away.

Chapter 2

The Global Ocean

Some people say that our planet has the wrong name. Instead of Earth, it should be called planet Water. After all, the world's oceans cover more than 70 percent of the earth's surface. That's 142 *million* square miles of water. It sure sounds like a lot of water, but how much is it really? The earth's oceans could cover the entire planet Mars in water not just once, but twice. The moon would be covered nine times. If you filled a standing pipe 75 miles in diameter with all the ocean water there is, those water molecules would climb 70,000 miles high. To give you an idea of how high that is, if you climbed to the top of that pipe, you'd be one-third of the way to the moon.

In fact, if you leveled the earth's surface both above and below the sea, so there were no peaks and no valleys, *everything* would sit 12,000 feet underwater. Water affects our weather, creates borders for our nations, continually changes the earth's surface, and as an ecosystem, it contains the most living things on the planet. It's the earth's trademark. Our oceans are a one-of-a-kind feature in the solar system. The temperature on the earth's surface is just within the range where water remains liquid. Below 32 degrees water freezes, and above 212 degrees it vaporizes into a gas. Now a range from 32 to 212 degrees may seem pretty broad, but if you compare those temperatures to the highs and lows throughout the universe, they're mild. It's a chilling zero degrees in space and in the tens of millions degrees on a star. The in-between temperatures where water can flow are actually pretty rare. They seem to exist only on earth. The rest of the universe is either frozen solid or flaming gas. Our oceans are unique, and we are more connected to them than you might think!

Is it true that humans evolved from ocean life?
Maybe. Our bodies are almost three-quarters fluid. The weird thing about our body fluid is that it's *very* similar to ocean water! Both have fats, proteins, carbohydrates, enzymes, hormones, and living cells. Both are a complex solution of dissolved solids and gases. For this reason scientists guess that our ancestors came right out of the sea. If you've ever seen photographs of a newly developed human fetus, you may have noticed that it looks a lot like a fish!

At four to five weeks old, a human fetus has six projections coming out of its neck area that scientists say look a lot like fish gills. It has a large head, and its body is like a tail. Tiny buds that will become hands and feet are used like flippers to swim in the amniotic fluid. Its eyes are just dark pits set in the sides of its skull, much like a fish.

What's in ocean water?

Every natural element that we know of on earth appears in the ocean, including gases, minerals, and dissolved solids. Of all the dissolved solids, there's the greatest amount of (you guessed it) salt. If you could take all the salt out of the ocean, it would dry into a mass the size of Africa. Imagine another continent on earth that was solid salt! Or if you'd rather spread it out, the 166 million tons of salt could cover all the continents with a 500-foot-thick salty crust. Where did all that salt come from? Over millions of years, the forces of wind and water have broken up rocks and worn down mountains. Salt leaches from the rocks above and below sea level into the ocean.

There's also a lot of calcium, potassium, and magnesium in the ocean. Even gold. If you could mine all the gold from the sea, everyone on earth would have a nine-pound sack of it.

What's the difference between an ocean and a sea?

We often use the words sea and ocean to mean the same thing. Both are bodies of saltwater, but oceans are larger. Actually, there's only one ocean. People have divided the *global ocean* into sections and named each area, but the global ocean is really 326 million cubic miles of interconnected saltwater that fills in the deep depressions in the surface of the earth.

There are five oceans that together cover 142 million square miles. The Pacific is the largest, covering 63 million square miles. The Atlantic

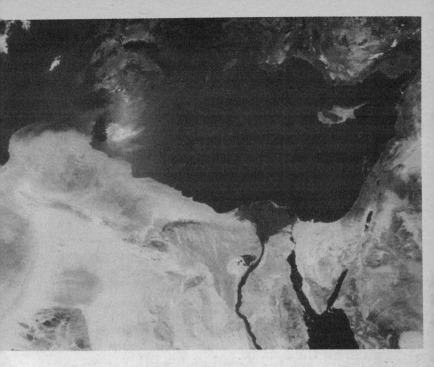

A satellite photograph showing an *enclosed sea*, the Mediterranean, in the upper center. The Nile River and part of the Red Sea are visible below it.

(National Oceanic and Atmospheric Administration)

covers 32 million, the Indian covers 28 million, and the Antarctic and Arctic are about the same size, covering 5 million square miles each. The remaining 9 million square miles are covered by the seas.

A sea is a smaller body of saltwater that may or may not connect with the ocean. The Dead Sea, the Caspian Sea, the Salton Sea, and the Sea of Azov have no outlet to the ocean. They are called *inland seas.* The Mediterranean is an *enclosed sea,* meaning it does connect to the ocean, but through a very narrow channel. The Mediterranean is almost landlocked by Asia, Africa, and Europe, therefore it can only flow into the Atlantic through the narrow Strait of Gibraltar. The North Sea is a *partly enclosed sea.* It connects to the ocean through a wider channel. Oceanographers say there are fifty-four enclosed and partly enclosed seas.

What are the seven seas?

Before the fifteenth century, the *seven seas* referred to the Red Sea, the Mediterranean Sea, the Persian Gulf, the Black Sea, the Adriatic and Caspian seas, and the Indian Ocean. But today, the seven seas refers to the world's oceans: the Arctic, the Antarctic, the Indian, the North and South Atlantic, and the North and South Pacific.

Why is the ocean blue?

The open ocean looks blue because of the sun shining on microscopic particles in the water. Near the shore, there are more floating plants. These plants have a yellow pigment in them. When yellow mixes with blue, what do you get? The green water you see near land. But blues and greens are not the only colors of ocean. Certain algae bloom in the Red Sea making the surface water red. The Yellow Sea gets its color from yellow mud that's washed into the sea from rivers. The Black Sea looks black because there's a lot of a hydrogen sulphide in the water and not much oxygen.

What does the bottom of the ocean look like?

Let's start with the area that borders the continents and work our way out and down to the deep, open ocean. The water-covered area that borders the continents is called the *continental shelf*. Along the coasts of the United States, this area covers about 1.6 million square nautical miles. *Nautical miles* are sea miles. They're how we measure distance over the ocean. When you measure long distances on land, you're counting *statute miles*. They're not the same thing. One square nautical mile equals 1.35 square statute miles.

The continental shelf is not a straight shelf like you'd see on a bookcase. It's a surface that slopes out from the shore an average of thirty miles and down to about 600 feet deep or less. This irregular shelf also has hills and canyons—a topography all its own.

At a depth of about 600 feet, the land surface beneath the water gets much steeper. Here starts the *continental slope*. In some places this slope is wider than others and it has a range of 12 to 62 miles. The continental slope is made of *sediment,* which is a mixture of natural debris. In this case it's mostly mud. Mud makes up about 60 percent of the recipe, sand 25 percent, gravel and rocks 10 percent, and shell fragments 5 percent. Most of the sediment is runoff from the continental shelf. The slope ends at anywhere from 4,900–11,000 feet. Now it may sound like we've covered a lot of territory already, but actually only 7 percent of the total ocean is shelf and 8 percent is slope. There's

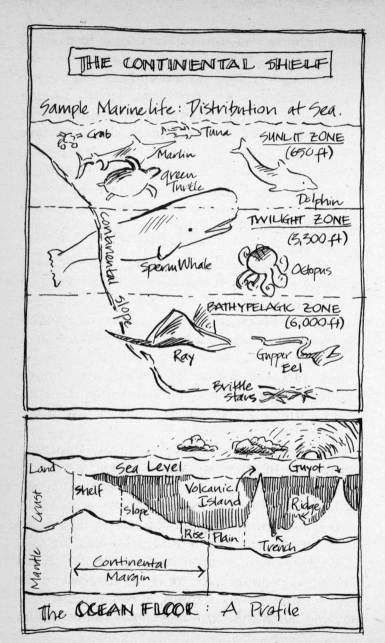

Examples of marine life that live on the three levels of the continental shelf (top). The geography of the ocean floor (bottom).

still another 85 percent of the ocean bottom to explore!

The next piece is the *continental rise*. This name is a little misleading. The ocean is still getting deeper—the surface bottom isn't rising higher. But if you look at this section from the point of view of the deep ocean floor, it's where the bottom begins to rise slightly before it makes a more dramatic climb at the slope. Its width is anywhere from 1 to 370 miles. The entire area that includes the continental shelf, slope, and rise is called the *continental margin*.

So we've finally come to the deep ocean floor—and I mean deep. All over the world, the depth of the ocean ranges from 9,000–13,000 feet. But don't picture a curved bowl like the bottom of a swimming pool. The ocean floor is an uneven terrain of mountains and valleys, like you'd find above sea level. In fact, the world's longest mountain range is on the bottom of the ocean. It's called the Mid-Atlantic Ridge, and it spans 59,000 miles in the middle of the Atlantic Basin.

To give you an idea of the size of these undersea mountains, think of this: at 29,028 feet high, Mt. Everest is the highest mountain above sea level. Yet the entire Mt. Everest would fit neatly into the deepest known part of the ocean. The Mindanao Trench, east of the Philippine Islands, is a huge depression in the western Pacific that's 35,800 feet deep. It could hold Mt. Everest in its belly with another 1¼ miles of water on top. By now, you get the picture—the deep ocean floor is a vast space. It's ⁵⁄₇ of the total sea area or half of the earth's total surface.

The bottom of the ocean has been compared to the surface of the moon. Potato-sized *nodules* are one of the things that give the ocean floor its moon-like quality. These nodules are lumps of man-ganese, cobalt, iron, and nickel. Scientists don't fully understand how these nodules form, but they do know that is happens over a very long period of time. The strange part is that these nodules only form around certain materials, and it's an odd se-lection. Bits of clay, shark's teeth, or the ear bones of whales that died ages ago are the base of these mysterious growths.

Sediment in the ocean originally comes from the land. Rivers, wind, and waves wash soil and rocks into the sea. Ash and lava from volcanic eruptions settle in the ocean. The remains of the sea's animal life mixes in also. All these elements create sed-iment that's continually moved in the ocean by currents, wind, and ice.

But where did all the water come from?

Billions of years ago, after the earth was born, it began to cool. As it cooled, what had been a gas condensed into a liquid on the planet's surface. Volcanoes inside the earth erupted and water came out from the interior to the surface. Over time, rocks eroded and salt was carried down into the oceans from the rivers.

The water in the ocean can be divided into lay-ers. The top layer is the warmest because it gets the heat of the sun. Below the surface is a denser, colder layer that's about 50 degrees. The top warmer layer and this colder layer underneath don't mix well. The point where they meet is called the *thermocline*. As you travel below the thermocline, the water gets gradually colder, down to about 35–37 degrees on the ocean bottom. Another way of thinking about the deep ocean is to think of two regions—the zone of light and the zone of perpetual darkness. The *zone of light* goes down to about 600 feet. Below that, there's not enough sunlight for green plants to do their act—to perform the magic of *photosynthesis*. That's when green plants use sunlight to form sugars and starches. These enriched plants become food for the little fish who become food for the big fish, and so goes the chain of life in the sea. Below 600 feet in the *zone of perpetual darkness* no light penetrates, but life still exists. It can be eerie to imagine life in a land of darkness—in the realm of sea monsters and other mysterious creatures of the deep where it's hard to separate fact from imagination. It's pretty amazing that anything exists down there at all, but there definitely is life on the bottom of the ocean.

They're under a lot of pressure!

Water exerts a lot of pressure. In fact, 1 cubic foot of water weighs more than 60 pounds. For every 33 feet you go under water, almost 15 pounds of pressure per square inch is added. What all that translates into is this: creatures living 330 feet below sea level, still far from the ocean bottom, tolerate 150 pounds of pressure for every square

True or False

Before you read any further, have some fun guessing about life at sea. Answer these true or false questions now, and then again once you're finished reading this book. You'll be amazed at how much you learn.

1) Most of the earth's surface is covered with ocean.

2) There have been waves over 100 feet high.

3) If you're stranded at sea and have no freshwater, it's better to drink seawater than no water at all.

4) The longest anyone has ever survived at sea *alone* on a raft is two months.

5) You can tell if land is nearby even if you can't see it and have lost your way.

6) Flying fish can't really soar through the air, they just swim fast.

7) As long as a shark doesn't see you, you're safe.

8) Scientists have proven that there's no such thing as a sea monster.

9) Sometimes ships and crews vanish from the face of the earth and are never seen again. No one can explain why.

10) The most deadly creature in the sea is the shark.

Answers: 1)T; 2)T; 3)F; 4)F; 5)T; 6)F; 7)T; 8)F; 9)F; 10)F.

inch of body surface. Just multiply by 10 and you can see that at 3,300 feet down, creatures take 1,500 pounds of pressure. So, in the deepest parts of the ocean, at 33,000–36,000 feet below sea level, 7.5 *tons* of pressure pushes on every part of a creature's body. Yet, there's life down there. Could you imagine walking around with even 50 pounds of pressure pushing against you from all sides?

Fortunately, it's not a human concern. When you're out in a boat above the deep ocean, it's enough to know that it's cold and dark down there. What you really want to concentrate on is staying afloat. It's the oceans, currents, and tides that you have to be prepared for, so that the water doesn't take you anywhere you don't want to go.

Chapter 3

Wind, Waves, and Currents

Currents

Even if your only experience with boating is a ten-inch schooner in the bathtub, you know enough about life on the high seas to make some waves and test your little boat's seaworthiness. In other words, an ocean voyage means movement, and much of it is out of your control. True, you turn on the engine or set the sails and steer the boat, but the water sets its own pace. In fact, if you like to spend your summers swimming off Cape Cod, it's not exactly Massachusetts water you're swimming in. Those water particles have been on a long journey and may have come from as far away as Antarctica—a 9,000-mile trek.

But Why Does Water Move?

Water moves because of the rotation of the earth. The earth orbits the sun and revolves on its own axis. The sun's rays are most intense near the equator, so the surfaces of the seas near the equator are warmer than the sea surfaces near the poles. When water is heated, it expands. Near the equator, sea level is just a few inches higher than other places because of the expanded water. This creates a little slope. When you pour water downhill, it travels. In this case, it travels toward the poles where the water is very cold and heavy. The heavier, cooler water sinks below the warm water and spreads slowly on the bottom of the ocean. That's one reason water moves. The earth's rotation also makes water move by producing *ocean currents*. Currents can be cold or warm, and they vary in speed. Some seem hardly to move at all. Others move at almost 6 mph. The global ocean is constantly in motion trying to reach a kind of balance. Water that's very salty and dense moves toward water that's not as dense. It's all about trying to even things out and get to a state of *equilibrium*. It's a little like balancing the contents of your life. If you spend too many nights staying up late to read the latest mystery, you're too tired to play your best at baseball the next day. You have to balance your need for sleep, quiet times, and high-energy play. And that balance changes from year to year as you change. The ocean is in this ever-changing state also.

But that's not the whole picture. The earth is spinning at about 1,000 mph at the equator. That's pretty fast, so fast, that it spins right out from under the oceans. The earth spins toward the east. The water that's left in its tracks piles up on the oceans' western shores. At the same time, the air is affected by our planet's rotation. It moves also, and so we have wind patterns as well. These are the surface *wind currents*. Winds blowing across the water interact with the ocean currents to make quite a commotion at sea.

Wind

Wind is the most important weather condition for sailors to be aware of. It tells them what kind of conditions they'll be working in—and which to get out of. Tornadoes, hurricanes, and cyclones are wind systems every sailor wants to avoid. On land, obstacles like buildings and mountains block the wind, so it can be hard to tell which way it is blowing. On the open seas, however, there's nothing but water. A sailor can get a lot of information about developing winds by looking at the waves.

Waves

Ordinary waves are created by wind that blows over the surface of the ocean. Here's a little wave vocabulary that every sailor ought to know. The high point of the wave is called the *crest*. The low point is the *trough*. The distance from the crest of one wave to the crest of the next is the *wave length*. The distance from the crest down to the trough is the *wave height*. If you're watching the waves from a fixed point, like a boat dock, the time it takes for two crests to pass you is a *wave period*. All these terms help describe the different kinds of waves.

If you've ever visited the ocean, you and your friends have probably played in the waves. If so, you know that an exciting moment for a strong swimmer is when the wave comes crashing down and you ride it (or it takes you) to shore. Why do the waves come crashing down? As the wave comes into shallow water, it gets shorter and slower. The water that makes up the wave gets pushed up and the wave gets taller. The crest of the wave is now going faster

WAVE AT SEA

Crest

Trough

wave height

wave length

On the open sea, waves form peaks, or crests. The height of a wave is measured from the bottom of the dip, or trough, to the top of the crest. The wave length is the distance from crest to crest.

than the rest of it, outrunning the water under it. Then it crashes down. We call these *breakers.* When the wave breaks the water rushes up onto the beach. That's called the *uprush,* and it's what demolishes your sandcastle. Then the water flows back again, and that's called the *backwash.*

These *surface waves* are usually less than 12 feet high. In really bad storms, there are waves over 50 feet. Under certain conditions they can get a lot higher. The highest open-ocean wave ever recorded was 112 feet high. That's not quite as high as the Statue of Liberty, but almost! The wave was mea-

WAVES HITTING SHORE

Breakers

Uprush

Backwash

When the crest of a wave crashes down, you get breakers. Then the water rushes on shore—that's the uprush.
Next is the backwash, when the water flows back into
the sea.

sured in 1933 by an American tanker traveling from
Manila to San Diego in a 68-*knot* windstorm. A knot
is one nautical mile, so that's 6,112 feet an hour.

The most serious waves, the ones disaster movies
are made of, are *tsunami*. The word tsunami is Japanese for harbor wave. When these waves overflow
onto the land, we call them *tidal waves*.

Tsunami are caused when the ocean floor or the
shore line moves in a big way. That means volcanic

eruptions, earthquakes, and landslides. There are volcanoes on the ocean floor. If one erupts, gases escape and push the water up into a dome shape. When the disrupted water settles back down, it creates a wave. This is no ordinary wave. It's only 2–3 feet high, but the wave length is over 100 miles and it's moving over 400 knots or about 500 statute miles an hour. When it gets into shallow water, it rushes onto shore at a destructive speed. The worst tsunami occurred in 1883 when the volcano of Krakatau between the islands of Sumatra and Java blew up. The waves that hit the shore were 115 feet high. One thousand villages were swept away, and 36,000 people were killed. Most tsunamis occur in the Pacific Ocean. Luckily, such disasters don't happen very often. In Japan, a wave 25 feet high is recorded only once every fifteen years.

Different Kinds of Tides

If you've ever hunted for seashells by the ocean, you probably know that sometimes the water recedes from the shore leaving thousands of shells available for the taking. That's *low tide*. At other times of the day, the water comes much farther up onto the beach. That's *high tide*.

There are actually three categories of tides. On the east coast of the United States, in places like Florida and Massachusetts, the tides are *semidiurnal*, meaning the tides rise and fall twice every day. On the coast of China, there are daily or *diurnal* tides. That means there's one high tide and one low tide each day. On the Pacific coast of the United States, in places like California and Oregon, the tides are *mixed*. That means there are two low tides and two high tides each day, but the two high tides reach different highs and the low tides reach different lows.

Why Tides Exist

What causes the water to rise and fall like this? Basically, it's pulled by the forces of the sun and moon. All of the earth's surface feels the powerful attraction of the moon and sun, but the land can't respond by moving. Water, being in a fluid state, can. Thus, we have tides.

Since the moon is closer to the earth than the sun, it has the greatest effect on the tides, even though the sun is over two million times the size of the moon. The moon's monthly cycle influences the height of the tides. During the new moon and the full moon, the earth, the sun, and the moon are lined up together. So, the forces of the sun and moon combine to create the highest high tides for the month. These are called the *spring tides* because the tides seem to spring right up from the sea.

During the first and third quarters of the moon, the earth, sun, and moon make a different formation. Each takes the corner of a triangle. Then the pull of the sun works against the moon. The highest tides, called *neap tides*, are lower.

Generally, high tides are two to ten feet high, but in a few places they can get much higher. The highest tides in the world are in the Bay of Fundy, in Canada, between Nova Scotia and New Brunswick. An area called the Minas Basin is at the head of the bay. About one hundred billion tons of water goes in and out of the bay twice each day. That much water rises into a tide fifty-three and a half feet high. That's definitely not a place you want to go sailing into!

The ocean probably seems vast and unpredictable. You need to know about the nature of the ocean so you're prepared to handle different situations and so you know which to avoid. You can't control what the ocean does, but you can know how to take care of yourself. In this case, that means knowing how to safely operate your boat and what to do in an emergency.

Chapter 4

Safety at Sea

Now that you know something about the nature and habits of the sea you sail on, let's talk about your boat. If you're taking a trip on an ocean liner you can rely on the ship's crew to ensure your safety. But even if you know nothing about boating, it's still your responsibility to find out what kind of emergency equipment and boating experience your captain has. If friends invite you out on their sailboat for the weekend, ask them if they're prepared to handle mishaps. Usually, you're sailing in an area where there's frequent boat traffic. You're probably on a lake in a recreation area where it's easy to contact another boat by radio when you need help. In other words, have fun. You're not likely to get into a real survival situation.

Boating on the open seas is another matter. You can end up far from help, and let's face it, the water can get pretty rough. Many sailors find themselves in survival situations because of sharks or whales damaging their boats. That won't happen to you on a mountain lake, but out in the Pacific, be prepared!

Tips for Safe Boating

If you're learning to operate a boat, here are some safety tips:

- Take a course in safe boating. Contact a local marina or sailing school to find out about what's available in your area. The U.S. Coast Guard Auxiliary, the volunteer civilian section of the Coast Guard, offers free seamanship courses to the public. There are several different classes, including a *Young People's Boating* course for kids ages eight to fifteen. Call your local Coast Guard office for information.
- If you have a power boat, know how much gas your fuel tank holds and how far it will take you.
- Be sure you know how to use the distress signals in your emergency kit described below.
- Make sure all nonswimmers wear flotation devices.
- If your boat capsizes but it's still floating, stay with it.
- Have a good anchor and enough line to keep your boat steady in heavy winds.
- On small boats, be sure you have a second engine, paddles, or oars in case your engine breaks down or there's no wind to sail by.
- Learn weather warning signals.
- Make sure at least one other person knows how to handle your boat in case you get sick or hurt.

Salty Talk

If you want to sound like a real sailor, you have to know the language. Here are a few nautical terms to get you started.

About—to go the opposite way. If the captain says Come about, it means you're going to turn the boat around.

Ballast—heavy material like iron or stone that's put in the bottom of the *hold* to keep the ship steady.

Below—under the deck. When you go into the boat's cabin you're going *below.*

Bow—the rounded, forward part of the vessel.

Capsize—to overturn.

Davy Jones—an old sea term that refers to the spirit of the sea. *Davy Jones's locker* is the bottom of the sea.

Dead Reckoning—figuring out the ship's position by following its course and distance as recorded in the ship's log.

Dinghy—small open boat, usually used to hold supplies or to row out to your boat's mooring.

Draft—the depth of water a boat needs to float.

Even Keel—when the boat sits evenly on the water. Neither end is lower than the other.

Fathom—nautical term used to measure depth. A fathom is six feet.

Fore and Aft—refers to the length of the ship. *Fore* is the front half and *aft* is the back.

Galley—like a ship's kitchen. The place where the cooking is done.

Helm—all the steering machinery, such as the tiller, rudder, and wheel.

Hold—the inside of the ship where the cargo is stowed.

Horizon—where the sea meets the sky. The distance of the horizon depends on where you stand. When you stand on shore, the horizon is about 2.5 miles away. On a cliff one hundred feet high, it's about 12 miles away. You can't see beyond the horizon because the earth is round. The sea just curves right out of sight!

Hull—the body of the boat.

Land Ho!—the cry used when you first see land after you've been at sea.

League—once used to measure distance. A league was about 3.4 miles.

Port—the left side of the ship as you look forward.

Schooner—a boat with two or more masts. A *sloop* has one mast.

Scull—to propel the boat with one oar at the stern.

Starboard—the right side of the boat looking forward.

Stern—the back end of the vessel.

Topsides—the part of the boat from the waterline to the rails.

- Maintain your emergency equipment well. Teach passengers how to use it. It won't help you if it's broken or you don't know how to use it.

- Before you leave shore, give a responsible person on shore your *float plan*. This plan lets him or her know your basic route, stopovers, and arrival or return. If you do have an accident, you'll know just how many days it will be until someone starts looking for you.

Knots

On a boat, and in any survival situation, it's important to know how to make a good knot. You make knots when you rig up a spear or net for fishing. You use knots to make a canopy for shelter from the sun. You make knots to tie your solar still for fresh water onto the boat. You'd be amazed at how many times you make knots, and a weak knot could mean a near-fatal loss of some valuable equipment. Even in ordinary circumstances, any sailor will be knotting lines. So get out your rope and practice. Just follow the diagrams and in time, you'll get the hang of it. The descriptions of the knots below tell you when to use which knot.

Square Knot. Use a square knot when you want to tie the ends of two ropes together. The ropes should have about the same diameter. In other words, don't try to tie a thin cord and a heavy rope together by this method. You'll regret it when your precious cargo goes drifting off without you. But a square knot with equal ropes can be depended on. The knot will actually get tighter when it's pulled. One more word

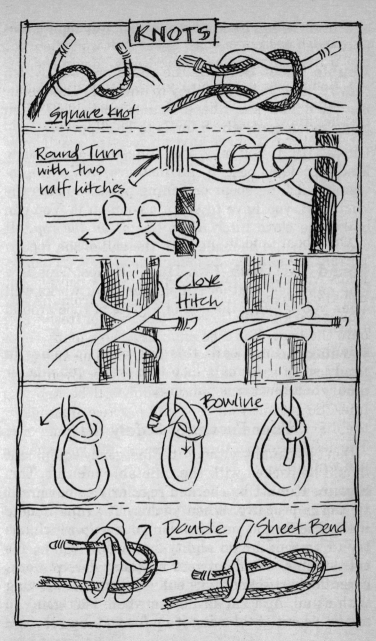

The most common knots that sailors use to secure their boats and belongings. These will help you in many wilderness situations.

of caution: a square knot made with wet ropes probably won't hold.

Double Sheet Bend. If the ropes are wet, which they're likely to be, or if they're unequal in diameter, use the double sheet bend. It also works well when tying nylon cord, which tends to be slippery.

Clove Hitch. You may need to fasten rope to some kind of pole or post, if, for instance, you're improvising a fishing spear or fishing pole. To make the knot hold, you have to keep tension on it. You can make the clove hitch *at any point on the rope*. It doesn't have to be made with the end of the rope.

Round Turn with Two Half Hitches. This is a long name for a rather simple knot that works well when you're tying the *end* of a piece of rope around a post.

Bowline Knot. Learn this one well. It comes in handy since it forms a loop that won't get smaller even when tension is put on it.

Your Essential Safety Kit

Don't be caught without it! Emergency equipment should be packed with the inflatable life raft. This equipment must be checked regularly to be sure it all works properly. When you're out in the middle of the Pacific and you abandon your ship which has been damaged by an eighty-foot sperm whale, it's not the time to find out your air pump doesn't work. Even the best set of lungs will have trouble blowing the raft up. And I'm afraid the whale isn't going to say he's sorry by blowing it up for you. Be sure you have the items listed below and that they're in good working condition. Know how to use them. Pack them well in plastic. Steve Callahan is a naval architect whose twenty-one-foot sailing cruiser, the *Napoleon Solo,* sank after it was hit by what was probably a whale. He was adrift in the Atlantic in a five-and-a-half-foot inflatable raft for seventy-six days. He had only three pounds of food and eight pints of water; he survived by his ingenuity, eating raw birds and fish he caught mostly with a makeshift spear. He drifted 1,800 miles and was the only man to survive more than a month at sea in an inflatable raft alone. He lived to write about his harrowing experience, so I guess you could say he's an expert. Here's what he recommends:

- 6 pints of water in tins with lids. The tins can be reused for storage.
- 2 solar stills to turn seawater into fresh water for drinking.
- food, for those days when the fish swim off with your bait. Pack nutritious, canned items like peanuts, baked beans, and soaked raisins. Canned foods will stay dry until you have to eat them.
- can opener.
- fishing kit with 50 feet of twine and 3 medium hooks.
- a fishing net.
- sheath knife and pocket knife.
- short spear gun.

- 100 feet of heavy rope or line.
- space blanket, which is a shiny, thin foil that traps your body heat and reflects it back onto you. It can get very cold out there.
- air pump to inflate the raft and to pump it back up as leaks develop.
- raft patching kit with glue, rubber patches, and screw-like plugs.
- 2 sponges to mop up water.
- 2 short wood paddles to drive off sharks.
- 2 hand-launched parachute flares to signal passing ships and planes.
- 3 hand-held red flares and 3 orange smoke flares also for signaling.
- flashlight and 2 signal mirrors and a distress lantern. (see chapter 8 for the uses of different distress signals.)
- survival charts, books, pencils, erasers, and paper.
- first aid kit (see chapter 9 for contents).
- dry socks for each passenger in a plastic bag.
- plastic bags, because all of this stuff will serve you better if it's dry.

Your boat should also have extra canvas sheeting that you can use for protective covering and a ship-to-shore radio.

I hope you'll never have to use these items, except in practice. But even the best sailors can't control the forces of nature. Strong winds, waves, and

Survivors of the *Malay*, a tanker damaged by shellfire and torpedoes from a German submarine during WWII. Afire and badly damaged, *Malay* ran toward Norfolk, VA where it reached safety. Four men were lost and three injured.

(Life-Saving Museum of Virginia, Virginia Beach, Virginia).

whales can set you on a survival adventure that will change the way you look at life forever. In 1972, one family of five by the name of Robertson plus one crew member set out to sea in a nineteen-ton, forty-three-foot schooner. That's a big boat. Yet, it happened to them.

Here's what could happen to you: You're sailing on the ocean blue, watching the sunlight dance on the water, inhaling the salty, sea air, and BAM! A whale rams the side of your boat and she starts to

Some "Can You Believe It?" Shipwrecks and Other Sea Stories

If you think the Baileys' adventure was unbelievable, check out these other *true* stories.

- Twenty-five-year-old Poon Lim, a Chinese steward, holds the record for the longest survival at sea. He was afloat alone on a life raft with rations for 50 days. Yet he survived from November 23, 1942 until April 5, 1943. He was rescued after 133 days. He used the spring from his flashlight to catch fish and caught seabirds with his hands.

- The record for the longest survival at sea with no support goes to a Norwegian seaman. He fell from a freighter in the Gulf of Mexico and spent thirty hours in the water with no raft, no lifejacket, nothing. He was finally rescued by a tanker.

- James Dugan, a member of one of Jacques Cousteau's sea expeditions, witnessed a short but very strange survival story. He saw a diver being swallowed by a giant grouper fish—and then escape by squirming out through the fish's gill.

- Perhaps the weirdest story of all involved a British seaman named James Bartley in 1891. He was a harpooner on a whaling ship. A wounded whale hit his boat. All of the other sailors jumped off the boat in time, but Bartley got whacked by the whale's tail. He flew into the air and landed in the whale's mouth. He was engulfed in a great darkness and slipped along a smooth passage. Then, he was in a sack much larger than his body that was very hot and dark. He couldn't see anything, but with his hands he felt fish squirming around. Meanwhile, his shipmates watched while Bartley was swallowed alive by an eighty-foot sperm whale.

The next day, the sailors saw the same wounded whale dead in the water. They removed the whale blubber in the usual way, which took forty-eight hours. When they got to the whale's stomach, they saw a writhing human form. They cut in quickly and there was Bartley, covered in whale blood, his face purple and twisted.

He recovered enough after two weeks to tell his story. Then he lived another eighteen years, but his skin remained pure white as it had been bleached by the acid in the whale's stomach. He never went to sea again.

- Sea creatures can sometimes *help* humans in a survival situation. In 1969, a young South Korean sailor fell overboard. He climbed onto a passing sea turtle who carried him for over a hundred miles. The turtle never once dived underwater. The sailor was rescued after fifteen hours on the turtle's back.

sink. You try desperately to bail out the water that rushes in even though you know it's useless. Within moments you abandon ship and get into your trusty life raft. You sit in these tubes of rubber, exhausted and stunned, watching the remains of your beautiful craft disappear into the ocean.

Then all is quiet and calm again. The sea knows nothing of your plight. You're just a little speck of life in the immense ocean. Everything is as it was, except for one small detail. You're no longer a speck merrily on your way in a sleek schooner. You're a speck going nowhere in a clammy raft. And then the question hits: *Now what do I do?* True, the Robertson family was rescued and brought home safely after thirty-eight days adrift. But as you pull the supplies floating in the water into your life raft, home seems a galaxy away.

Chapter 5

Shelter at Sea

Help! What Do I Do Now?

Don't panic. You're scared, and that's natural. You're adrift at sea, and as much as you love the water, it's not your natural habitat. Fear of the unknown is a big obstacle. Just solve each problem one by one, and none of them will be as bad as you thought. Remember the survival stories you've heard. There are lots of them. Many people have lived for weeks at sea after a shipwreck. Their long ordeals are the exception. Over half of the boats that end up adrift at sea for more than twenty-four hours reach safety within five days. It's unusual for any lifeboat not to be picked up within three weeks.

Anyone stranded at sea has the greatest survival tool available at all times—ingenuity. Since you were a baby, you've been picking up objects and seeing how many ways you can use them. It's a natural human drive to experiment and explore, and it's part of you. Just keep telling yourself, "I'm going to be okay. I'll just take things one step at a time. We'll all help each other. Sure I'm scared. That's normal. And I'm also a lot of other things, like inventive and full of life. Someday I may even write a book about this!"

What To Do First

Protect yourself from the elements. In this case, that means the water, the wind, the baking sun, and the biting cold. As soon as you can, get as dry as possible. Constant contact with saltwater irritates the skin, and wet clothes will chill you pretty fast. Squeeze out your wet clothes, but put them back on unless it's warm out and the wind is mild. In that case, dry them layer by layer in the sun. Then put them back on for protection against sun and wind.

Take Care of Your Feet

Take off your shoes and socks, and dry them as well as you can. Hopefully, you have an extra pair of dry socks in your safety kit. If it's wet on the bottom of the raft, put your shoes back on. Why all this concern about your feet? Your feet may be sitting in cold water a lot of the time, so they're at risk for immersion foot, an uncomfortable condition I'll say more about in chapter 9. Try to keep the floor of the raft dry by bailing and sponging. Cover it with canvas or cloth for insulation.

If the weather is cold, huddle together with the rest of your crew. Spread any extra tarp or sailcloth over everyone. Steve Callahan hacked off a piece of the mainsail from his boat for cover. After his boat went down, cushions were left floating in the water. He retrieved these and sat on them to insulate his buttocks.

Don't Try Marathon Swimming, But Do Exercise!

Do easy exercises to keep your circulation going. That way, you'll feel warmer. Exercise your toes and fingers, your shoulders and buttocks—areas that tend to chill and stiffen up. Every so often, raise your feet up for a minute. Even move your face muscles. The movement will help prevent frostbite. It's pretty confined in a life raft, so your knees and back will soon feel cramped. Stretch out whenever possible.

Too Cold...or Too Hot?

Stretching and mild exercise are important even if it's not cold. In fact, it may be quite hot. Daytime temperatures in the warm Pacific can reach eighty to ninety degrees. All that sun reflected on the water makes the heat intense. Exposure to the sun causes additional problems; it makes you thirstier, cuts down the amount of water in your body, and leaves you looking as red as the lobsters and crabs below.

Cover your skin to protect it from sunburn. Roll down your sleeves, wear a hat, and pull up your collar. If you have sunglasses, wear them. Don't forget about your eyelids, the back of your ears, and the skin under your chin. Put cream on them—they burn easily! Pour some seawater on your clothes. Don't drench yourself—just dampen them. As the water evaporates, it will cool you down.

Keep Covered

Whether it's sunny, cloudy, or raining, you need to protect your body from overexposure. Ideally, your raft has an attached canopy that forms a little roof to shield you from the elements and protect you from water spraying into the raft. Some rafts even have insulated floors and spray shields. If your boat doesn't have an awning, rig one up. Use a canvas sheet or whatever water-resistant fabric you have on hand. Tie it to the sides of the raft with rope. Use whatever you can to prop your canopy up in the middle. That way, it won't feel as stuffy inside the raft.

Housekeeping at Sea

Now that you're "settled," see what equipment you have available and what condition it's in. Waterproof as many items as you can by putting them in plastic bags. Certain things, such as compasses, watches, matches, and lighters, are greatly affected by salt-water, so protect those right away. Find your emergency radio and your signal devices.

Organize your equipment. Put all your food items in one area of the raft and your signal devices in another. That way you can grab what you need quickly. When a ship passes by, you won't want to waste precious time searching for your flares. You're hard to see out there among the waves, so no one will notice you unless you get their attention.

Check the raft for any leaks. It's better to fix them before they get bigger and before you start deflating. True, you can always pump up the tubes, but there's a lot to do when you're adrift at sea. You need to conserve your energy. Try to think ahead and cut down on extra work. You're probably not alone, but

RAFT
with SEA ANCHOR →
... A fish's eye view

The sea anchor drags underwater and helps control the rafts movement.

with family or friends. That makes a big difference. Not only can you boost each other's spirits, but you can share the work. Cooperation is very ecological; it's a great time and energy saver. Divide up jobs and then take turns at them. Today you may be food collector, tomorrow, bailer.

Throw out your *sea anchor,* or *drogue.* This serves several purposes. It will help keep you from drifting too fast, and since you have left a float plan with someone onshore, people know your approximate route to your destination. If you stay in the general area where you capsized, it will be easier for a rescue team to find you. Also, when you're drifting rapidly, it's a lot harder to catch fish. You'll get very hungry. What's more, the sea anchor adds some resistance to the waves and will help prevent waves from lifting the raft and flipping it over.

If you don't have a sea anchor, or if you lose it to some fish as the Baileys did, improvise. Use the raft case, a bail bucket, or even a bundle of clothes. The sea anchor is tied to the raft with rope. If you have enough cloth, wrap some around that rope so it doesn't chafe the raft and possibly cause a leak. Check for sharp edges on *anything* so the raft is not punctured accidentally. Keep your raft-patching kit handy. And if you run out of plugs and glue, check the first aid kit for bandaids and tape. You get the idea . . . use anything. If you have more than one raft, tie the rafts together. They will be easier for an aircraft to see.

If you haven't already done so, take your seasick pills. Even the most experienced sailors can get seasick in a raft. It's a very small craft and sits low in

Monster sidebar: A shadowy photograph of the legendary Loch Ness monster of Scotland.

(AP/Wide World Photos)

the water. You're in continual motion. The rubber and glue of the raft don't smell very good. The air that's trapped in the raft under the canopy gets stale and humid. You're probably not going to feel your best. The seasick pills will help you feel better and think more clearly. In a couple of days, if you're not rescued yet, you'll have adjusted to these new conditions. We humans are remarkably adaptable.

By now you should be safely adrift in your organized raft. You've taken an inventory of what you have to work with. You're about to undertake the survival adventure of a lifetime...but you're thirsty.

Sea Monsters and Mysterious

Appearances

The ocean is a vast, dark ecosystem with hidden depths. Strange things have appeared from the sea, and many things have disappeared into it. Here are a few of the puzzling and chilling mysteries of the deep.

- In August of 1817 there were strange sightings off Cape Ann near Gloucester, Massachusetts. For two weeks, hundreds of people saw the same thing. A dark brown creature fifty to one hundred feet long, with the head of a turtle or rattlesnake, was seen traveling through the water at about thirty miles an hour. It held its head out of the water for an hour at a time as it twisted and turned through the waves. Then it would sink like a stone back down into the water. This odd serpent was named the Gloucester Sea Monster.

- A similar creature has been spotted in Lake Champlain, between New York and Vermont. "Champ" is America's version of the Loch Ness monster. Champ is described as a grayish, forty-foot-long beast with a mane that goes from head to toe. It has horns or whiskers sticking out of its nostrils and swims at about fifteen miles an hour. Many reliable scientists, lawyers, and mariners still report Champ sightings.

. . . and Disappearances

- The mystery of the ship the *Mary Celeste* is one of the most puzzling in maritime history. She left New York in November of 1872 with Captain Benjamin Briggs, his wife and child, and a crew of seven. The ship was next seen on December 4, 600 miles west of Portugal. The *Mary Celeste* was in perfect condition but there was no one on board. One lifeboat had been launched, and the last ship's log was recorded ten days before. What happened to the crew? Why did they abandon a ship in good condition? Some say pirates kidnapped them, but there was no sign of violence, not even a bloodstain. Others say the crew was eaten by a giant squid, or taken by UFOs. There's a small museum in New York City all about this mystery.

- Many ships or crews have disappeared without a trace in an area of the Atlantic known as the Bermuda Triangle. If you drew a line from Miami to Puerto Rico and then to Bermuda, the space inside the borders is the place where over a hundred ships and planes and more than a thousand sailors and pilots have vanished. It's the most feared area in the seven seas. Here's why.

  In 1881, a schooner named the *Ellen Austin* was found in excellent condition, with no crew and a full load of timber. The captain of the ship that found the *Ellen Austin* put a full crew on board to sail her back. The two ships were separated in a storm. When they met again a few days later, the schooner was unharmed, but again, no crew. The captain put yet another crew on board. This time, both the crew *and* ship disappeared without a trace.

In a different incident, a ship washed ashore without a crew. The *Carroll A. Deering* was found in 1971 off Cape Hatteras, North Carolina. It was stuck on sands where there was no storm the night before. Everything was in place on board, with half-eaten plates of food set at the table. Weeks later, the ship was still in the sand. People ashore said they heard weird sounds, even screams, coming from it. Still, the ship was empty.

Most scientists today admit that the Bermuda Triangle is a strange, unexplained phenomenon. Are those missing people out there somewhere in space? Or could they be under the sea? Plato, a Greek philosopher, described a place called Atlantis. He claimed it was a place inhabited by very advanced people. Legend has it that the people of Atlantis conquered all the world by 9600 B.C., except Greece. Greece was saved when Atlantis was swallowed by the sea and became the lost continent.

Perhaps this is just a myth. But there have been other cities that were once considered mythical and then thousands of years later were discovered to have existed. What's more, the migratory patterns of certain birds and eels suggest that once these species came upon land in the middle of the North Atlantic. Migratory patterns of animals are passed on from memory to memory for generations. Do these creatures circle the seas looking for Atlantis?

Chapter 6

Water, Water, Water

Stop! Don't Drink!

"Water, water, every where, nor any drop to drink." So goes the famous poem, *The Rime of the Ancient Mariner,* by Samuel Coleridge. It's a strange paradox: there you are, living on the water, and yet dehydration is a serious risk.

But isn't drinking seawater better than drinking no water at all? Definitely not. Don't even mix it with fresh water. You might feel better at first because the sense of dryness in your mouth will go away. But in a short time, you'll regret it. Seawater introduces so much salt into your body, that it takes more fluid to wash it out than you put in. In other words, seawater is three times saltier than urine. So for every cup of seawater you drink, your body produces three cups of urine to flush out the salt. Urine is partly water. Where does your body get the water to make three cups of urine? From your body tissues, and that's dangerous because it can literally cause you to wither away. So if you drink seawater, you'll dehydrate three times as fast as you would have if you drank no water at all. In fact, here's a story to illustrate just how deadly a little seawater can be.

The crew of the *MV Mosfruit* was adrift for nine days in the North Atlantic Ocean. They had three dogs and a cat with them. They decided to give the animals the same ratio of water and dog biscuits that they themselves had of water and human food. All of the crew and dogs survived the nine days, but the cat died on the third day because she kept sucking saltwater off her fur.

Not from the Sea, but from the Air

Well, that probably convinces you to keep the ocean out of your mouth. But what do you drink instead? You have emergency water in your survival kit. Hold onto that for now. That's for when all else fails and you're absolutely desperate. First, try some other methods.

After you're settled in your raft, set yourself up to collect and store water. At night and on foggy days, fresh water in the form of dew will condense on the floor and sides of your raft. Lay a tarp down on the raft floor with the edges turned up to collect dew. Then you can lift this water up and pour it into a container to store. Taste it before you store it to make sure it hasn't been contaminated by salty sea spray.

Try to navigate towards rain clouds. They're the gray, spooky looking ones called *nimbus clouds*. Wipe out any *catchments* (water-catching containers) you'll use to catch the rainwater so they're not salty. Then sit out there in your poncho and let the rain bounce off your shoulders and roll down into

Nimbus **or rain clouds, ready to burst.**

your container. Long hair and moustaches are good rain collectors also. The water will drip off the ends of the hair so you can direct it into your tin. Why bother trying to catch it? Why not leave a cup just sitting there to do the work?

Try this experiment at home on a rainy day. Set two containers outside in a heavy rain. Put one in the middle of the driveway. Place the other under a roof overhang or someplace that the water runs off of. After an hour or so, which has more water in it? Probably the one under the runoff. Directing or funneling the rain will yield more water than just randomly catching drops.

Not a Cloud in the Sky

What happens if it doesn't rain? Good question. And luckily, there's an answer. Pull out the *solar still* that's in your survival kit. In tropical waters when it's calm and sunny, a working solar still will provide two pints of fresh water every day. That's enough for one person to get by for two days. If you have more than one still, get them all working at the same time.

Turning seawater into fresh water may sound like magic. When you're stranded at sea it *is* magic. Here's how it works. The solar still is attached to the raft with line and then lowered in the water to drag alongside the raft. It looks something like a balloon that inflates once it's in the water. Seawater pours into a reservoir on the top of the still. Then the salty water drains down a tube and drips onto a black cloth wick. This wick is suspended away from the sides of the balloon. It hangs inside a little hoop. The hoop is attached with line to the sides of the balloon. It's very important that the wick doesn't touch the sides of the balloon at all. Otherwise, salt from the wick will drain down into the balloon and contaminate the fresh water.

Where did the fresh water come from? The wick gets saturated with saltwater. Then some of that water evaporates leaving its salt content in the wick.

The water vapor condenses as little drops of fresh water on the sides of the balloon. The drops trickle down into collection bags and a miracle occurs— water, water everywhere, and now you do have some to drink!

Plan for Tomorrow

Even if your solar still collapses and doesn't work, all is not lost. You need about a pint of water a day to stay in reasonably good shape. Under normal conditions, you'd drink more. But if your still doesn't produce, you may be able to get a bare survival ration from dew. Even two to eight ounces a day will keep you alive. In fact, people in good health can go eight to twelve days with no water at all. But if you have no water, don't eat. In order to digest your food, your body needs water. If you haven't put any in, your body will take it out from your tissues. In chapter 8 you can read all about the effects of dehydration, a condition you want to avoid.

Ration the available water carefully. Estimate how long you think you'll be adrift. How many days will pass before the person ashore with your float plan will notify the authorities? Are you in an area where there's frequent and regular boat traffic? Is it likely that you'll be picked up soon? Make your best conservative guess. Weigh that with the chances of catching rainwater and the productivity of your still. Then drink as much water as you think you can afford to.

The Keeper of the Water

Someone should be the keeper of the water. You can rotate this job each day—it's a very important one. The keeper of the water doles out each person's daily rations. She or he keeps track of how much water each person is drinking so that everyone gets his/her fair share. You'll all be feeling pretty thirsty. It would be easy and natural to think that you haven't yet had your full ration, when actually you have. Each drink will go further if you hold it in your mouth for a while. Give your mouth a chance to get moistened, gargle a little for your throat, and then swallow every last drop. Really savor it. Now you know how precious a glass of water is. Your thirst is quenched. You settle back for a moment, when suddenly you hear a loud grumble. No, it's not a sea monster—it's your stomach. You're hungry. What is there to eat?

Educational Voyages

Write to these places for information on their trips, the kind of research they do, and any other resources or good tips they might have.

Caretta Project, Savannah Science Museum, 4405 Paulsen St., Savannah, GA 31405. Trips to study the habits of the loggerhead sea turtle in Georgia's barrier islands.

Cousteau Society, Project Ocean Search, 777 Third Ave., New York, NY 10017. Trips to study the ocean and the creatures in it.

Field Courses and Environmental Science, Continuing Education, American University, Washington, D.C. 20016. Courses on land and sea.

Field Courses in Marine Biology, Eastern Campus, Suffolk County College, Riverhead, NY 11901. Various scientific voyages.

Marine Mammal Protection, New England Workshop, Inc., c/o Provincetown Center for Coastal Studies, PO Box 826, Provincetown, MA 02657. Workshop on marine mammal protection.

Ocean Research & Education Society, 51 Commercial Wharf 6, Boston, MA 02110.

The Oceanic Society, 240 Fort Mason, San Francisco, CA 94123.

Sea Education Association, PO Box 6, Church St., Woods Hole, MA 02543.

Sea-Fari Natural History Expedition, H&M Landing, 2803 Emerson St., San Diego, CA 92106. Scientific voyages in Baja waters.

Places to Visit

Miami Seaquarium, Miami, FL. A sea "zoo" complete with killer whales.

Mystic Seaport, Mystic, CT. A reconstructed 19th-century port city. A popular attraction that takes you back in time.

National Maritime Museum, San Francisco, CA. Learn about navigation and see model ships.

Planet Ocean, Miami, FL. A great place to learn about every aspect of the ocean from currents to sharks. They even have a real iceberg you can touch. This place features unusual audiovisual presentations that really take you out to sea.

US Naval Memorial Museum, Washington, D.C. This one has the American Revolution submarine, the *Turtle.*

Chapter 7

Dining Out

Now I'm Hungry!

Of course you're going to get hungry. But even though your stomach is roaring at you, don't panic. You can survive for several weeks without food. True, you'll get very skinny, not to mention grouchy and weak, but you'll survive. People have lost more than half of their normal weight and still recovered. That means a person weighing 140 pounds could drop down to 70 pounds in a survival situation and then fully recover once rescued and nursed to health.

The world's record for losing weight when adrift is held by Ensia Tira. She drifted for thirty-two days on an open raft in the Indian Ocean. Her normal weight was 132 pounds. Five days after her rescue, after she'd had five days worth of food and drink, she weighed a mere 56 pounds. That's about the weight of an eight-year-old child.

Crew from the SS *Fort Lamy* were adrift in the North Atlantic in March. They survived thirteen days without food *or* water! Here's another surprising incident; Alain Bombard and Jack Palmer took a fourteen-day voyage attempting to live off the sea.

They also went for ten days out of the fourteen without any food or water.

Your Water Garden

So you can live through such an ordeal, but it's very unlikely that you'll have to. These cases are the exceptions. The sea is a virtual water garden of healthy foods. Every year, over 60 million tons of food is harvested from the sea. That's a tremendous bounty—and none of it would be possible without *plankton*. Plankton is the first link in the food chain of the deep blue sea. It takes 10,000 pounds of tiny, microscopic diatoms, a type of plant plankton, to feed 1,000 pounds of copepods, a kind of animal plankton. Those 1,000 pounds of copepods will feed only 100 pounds of little fish like smelt. The 100 pounds of smelt feed only 10 pounds of mackerel. The 10 pounds of mackerel feed tuna. Can you guess how many pounds of tuna it will feed? That's right, just one. So 10,000 pounds of plant plankton produces only one pound of tuna. That's not quite three cans, or say, six tuna salad sandwiches (not counting the bread and mayo). Or consider it tuna steak dinner for two. And do you know how much body weight you'd put on if you ate the whole pound yourself? One-tenth of a pound. That's very little weight gain for all that plankton. So what is this plankton stuff that's supporting all the life in the sea?

Plankton—the Grass of the Sea

By studying fossils, scientists hypothesize about the beginnings of life on earth. They think that life appeared in the sea about 3,500 million years ago. These first forms of ocean life, basically bacteria, were simple plants made of one cell. Because these life forms were, and are, so weak, they can only drift along in the current. They can't propel themselves. Thus comes the name plankton, which is from the Greek word planktos. It means to drift or wander.

Plankton are a floating or drifting layer of life in the top one hundred feet of the sea. Photoplankton is plant plankton. Zooplankton is animal plankton. Zooplankton live on photoplankton. Like plants on land, these plant microorganisms can convert sunlight into sugars and starches. They then become food for other sea life that lives in the darker regions of the ocean.

Plankton, or a plant form of it called *diatoms,* are what make the ocean look green. Green water means life-giving water to other sea creatures. Blue water that's caused by light scattered among water molecules is not as rich. In fact, blue water is to green water as a desert is to a pasture. If you were a fish, where would you rather be?

If you looked at a diatom under a microscope, which is the only way to see one, you'd discover that it's enclosed in a shell. It produces the shell from its own secretions. These shells can be round or elongated and have very intricate designs. When diatoms die, living plankton eats the shells of the dead diatoms. In a way, they recycle themselves.

Salty Appetizers

Plankton sustains ocean life. Indirectly, it sustains you. But how about directly? Can you eat it? Shipwrecked sailors have eaten plankton and give varied opinions of it. Some say it's edible, others say it tastes terrible. It's worth a try when you're really hungry. It won't make a meal, but it could be an unusual appetizer. Just be sure you have plenty of freshwater, because it's salty stuff.

Steve Callahan thought nylon stockings would be a useful item in a survival kit because they could be used to catch zooplankton. Just trail the stocking at night. The zooplankton come to the surface then, and will be caught in the nylon. Look through your catch and remove any broken tentacles from jellyfish that could sting your mouth.

Seaweed

Eating weeds may sound like a desperate measure, but actually, you do it all the time. That's right— you've probably eaten seaweed before. There are more than seventy-five different kinds of seaweed that are used for food by people around the world. Maybe you've been to a health food or Japanese restaurant and sampled a seaweed delicacy. In Japan it's an essential and very healthy part of the diet. Some seaweeds contain a lot of protein. All are rich in minerals. But even if you haven't eaten seaweed directly, there may be seaweed in your ice cream, candy bar, jelly, cheese spread, or salad dressing. It's frequently used as an ingredient in these foods, but you might not recognize its scientific name on the label.

At sea, leafy green, brown, or red seaweed can be eaten raw or dried in the sun. If you spot some near

A *shearwater*, gliding on air currents produced by the rise and fall of the ocean's waves. *(Dr. Michael Tove)*

the surface of the water, just pull it up. Sometimes you'll catch some when you fish. And sometimes you'll catch fish in it. Tiny crabs and shrimp may be among the weeds. These can be eaten raw. The seaweed should be washed and the saltwater squeezed out. Eat only a little at a time since it works as a laxative. That means it may give you diarrhea. Diarrhea is dehydrating because you eliminate a lot of body fluid. In other words, you're wasting water. So let your body get used to the seaweed by introducing it gradually into your diet.

Birds at Sea

When you think about finding food at sea, you usually look to the water. But actually, there's nourishment in the skies as well. Seabirds, like petrels, shearwaters, seagulls, noddies, and boobies may come right to you. *Shearwaters* usually fly low over the ocean. The rise and fall of the ocean's waves produces air currents, and the shearwaters use these currents to stay aloft. These are graceful birds, about twelve to fifteen inches long with slender wings. They often migrate for thousands of miles. When birds fly over the open ocean, there aren't many rest stops, so your raft provides a welcome place for them to perch.

The *blue-footed booby*, the kind of bird the Baileys encountered, is a tropical seabird about the size of a goose. It gets its name from its blue feet and its behavior. The name "booby" comes from the Spanish word *bobo*, which means "stupid fellow." This bird lacks the average animal's fear of humans, and it's very clumsy on land. As you saw from Maralyn's experience, they're very easy to catch.

When the bird folds its wings, you can grab it by the legs and kill it. That may sound brutal, but you're living in a survival state. You've probably eaten plenty of birds before, but they come already slaughtered and neatly packaged in the supermarket. Even if you're a vegetarian, this is a time when you don't have the luxury of deciding what to eat based on your personal values, or your taste buds for that matter. In the spirit of the Native Americans, you can thank the bird for the life it's giving you. And as you say your thanks you must quickly kill and skin the bird. Survivalists recommend skinning over plucking. It's faster, and that way you remove the oil glands.

These *bluefooted boobies*, tropical seabirds, lack the average animal's fear of humans.

(Dr. Michael Tove)

Sailors stranded in the North Atlantic trailed some flying fish on a line to attract birds. The sailors grabbed the bird as it pounced on the fish. Then the bird was killed, skinned, and cut in half. One half was eaten raw, the other half was left out in the sun to dry and was eaten the next day. The bird's blood is not only nourishing but it will quench your thirst. The intestines will make good fish bait.

Now is probably a good time to talk about *plate fright*. If the idea of plankton and raw seagull is turning your stomach inside out, that's pretty normal. But in a survival situation, you have to work with what's available. Some people stranded on land or water have been known to starve to death because they couldn't bring themselves to eat foods they're not accustomed too. There will be plenty of opportunities for pizza and french fries when you get back home. In fact, you'll enjoy them more than you can imagine after your ordeal at sea. For now, pretend that bird is Thanksgiving dinner and eat heartily.

Hey, What About the Fish?

Yes, fish will be the foundation of your diet. Catching them will require ingenuity and energy, but the rewards in your belly are great. Fish tales will add some jawdroppers to the adventure stories you'll have to tell when you get back to school.

Before you get started with the real work of catching fish, how about a treasure hunt? Here's your clue: A tasty snack could easily be found if you were to turn your raft around. I don't mean changing it from west to east, but from right side up to upside down. Did you get it? The bottom of your raft may be sprouting food at this very moment.

Gooseneck barnacles are a kind of small clam that some sailors claim is delicious. The black bodies of the young barnacles are shelless and can be eaten raw. The long stalks are full of water. Triggerfish eat them off the bottom of the raft, and so can you. There are other reasons to eat the barnacles besides the fact that they're tasty. They slow down the movement of the raft, so if you're trying to navigate at all, barnacles are a hindrance. Also, they're part of a developing food chain. Barnacles attract trigger-

A *flying fish* (eronautes speculiger), in the tropical Atlantic, gliding through the air after leaping from the water. *(American Museum of Natural History)*

fish that attract dorados that attract sharks. So get rid of the barnacles. Mix some with rainwater for a crunchy soup.

Who's Out There?

The most common fish you'll find in the open sea are flying fish, triggerfish, and doradoes. *Flying fish* do exactly that. They have been known to leap out of the water and through the air at thirty-five miles an hour. At night, they may even land right in your raft.

Triggerfish are about twelve inches long. They

A Queen _triggerfish_. Note the little mouth and small flippers. *(Paul Humann)*

have little mouths with strong teeth and small flippers. They often peck at the bottom of the raft but rarely do any damage. A thick, horny bone protrudes on their backs. Their skin is quite tough, something like cowhide, and rough to the touch. The brownish-red blood is nourishing. Triggerfish meat may be a little bitter but very edible. Leftovers can be dried. Drying fish is quite easy. Just rig up a line and hang the fish from it. The sun will do the rest of the work.

Doradoes are bigger fish that eat triggerfish. They're usually about three to four feet long and weigh twenty to thirty pounds. An occasional whopper may be six feet long and weigh sixty pounds.

That's a lot of meat—and a lot of work to catch. Doradoes are noted for their bright yellow-finned tails and their agility. They leap right out of the sea in arcs up to ten feet high. If you have good aim, a spear gun is an effective way to catch one.

You probably remember that the Baileys practically lived on turtle meat. Sea turtles may even be found asleep right on the surface of the sea. Pulling one onto your raft and killing it takes muscle, but not a lot of skill. The Bailey method of killing a turtle was to hit the turtle's head until it was unconscious, then they cut the throat.

How to Catch Fish at Sea

Step One—Hooks and Lines. It's best if you have fishing line and hooks right in your safety kit. But if you don't, or if they've been lost in your fishing efforts, you can improvise. Check the first aid kit and everyone's pockets for safety pins, needles, or earrings with hooks. Fashion your best choice into a hook. See if you have a piece of wood—just two inches long will be big enough. Cut a notch in the end of it and place the hook in it. Tie the hook on securely with a shoelace or thread from someone's clothing.

Next, attach the hook, which is imbedded in the wood, onto a line. The line has to be strong because you're intending to catch some big doradoes that will last you awhile. Take a piece of canvas. Use a sharp knife to cut along the weave of the fabric. Then you'll be able to draw out strands of the fabric that are

Sections of twine strands twisted together make a secure fishing line.

about a yard long. When you have about ten canvas strands, fasten them together at one end. Have someone hold the fastened end. Now divide the open end in two. That is, hold five strands of canvas thread in each hand. You'll twist each section clockwise separately, but at the same time.

The next instruction is a little tricky, but you can do it. (Practice at home with yarn before you head out to sea.) As you twist each of the two sections clockwise, pass the section in your right hand counterclockwise around the section in your left hand. Twist the strands tightly in each section. Wind the sections together firmly. This way, it won't unravel when you're finished. The result is a line that can easily hold one hundred pounds without breaking. Your improvised line can definitely handle that dorado. If you have no canvas, unravel a rope and retwist in the manner described. Even the ravellings of someone's pant leg could be used.

Step Two—Bait and Lures. Now that you have a sturdy line, you need some bait. One place to look is under your raft. Small fish like to gather under it as the raft provides shade. To catch these little fish, use a net. If you don't have a net, you know what to do. Improvise. Make a net by tying some fabric around a circular frame. Make the hoop-shaped frame with any sturdy material like a bent piece of metal or plastic. You can scoop up small fish, shrimp, and crabs. The organs of fish that you've already eaten make excellent bait also.

You can lure fish to you at night by shining a flashlight on the water. You can even reflect moonlight onto the water with a mirror. Fish are attracted to bright objects. Some tinfoil stuffed with a little canned meat from your supplies makes good dorado bait. Large fish should be killed outside of the raft if possible by a blow to the head. A big, live fish flailing around in your raft could damage it . . . or you!

Using a Spear. Another way to catch fish, especially large ones, is with a spear. You can make an effective spear tip by tying a piece of pointed metal or sharp-

A pair of *doradoes*, the larger fish that feed on triggerfish. *(Tom Smoyer, Harbor Branch Oceanographic Institute)*

ened bone to a stick. You can also use your knife blade. Before you do, think carefully. Every time you fish you risk losing your spear, or damaging it. Of course, if you don't fish, you'll go hungry. But if you lose your spear, you may go hungry too. Still, if that's your only knife, it may be wiser to use something else for a point, or stick to lures. You'll need that knife to cut rope and clean fish.

If you have good aim, you can throw your spear at a fish that's airborne. *Be sure the spear is tied to the raft with some long rope.* If you miss, or the fish gets away, that's the end of some precious equipment. When you spear a fish in the water, wait patiently until it comes close enough for a good hit. If you only superficially wound the fish it can swim away. Now you have an enemy nearby. A strong dorado may come back and butt your raft all night. The next day you may be much too tired and aggravated to catch anything!

Once you spear a fish and disable it, you have to haul it into your raft. It will probably still be alive.

Fishy Trivia

Did you know that:

- a prehistoric fish called the coelacanth that was supposed to be extinct fifty million years ago showed up on the South African coast in 1938? What else is lurking down there from the days of the dinosaurs?

- in 1980, a paleontologist found the skull and teeth of an ancient walking whale? This 500-pound, 7-foot-long creature fed underwater during the day and walked in the marshes of Pakistan at night.

- the largest sea or land animal that ever lived is still alive? It's the sulphur bottom or blue whale. One of these giants reached 110 feet long and weighed about 200 tons. That's more than fifty elephants and twice as big as the largest known dinosaur!

- the giant squid has the largest eye of any animal? Tonight at supper, take a good look at your dinner plate. The eye of this squid is just a little bigger.

- the largest sea turtle ever recorded was in the Pacific? This leatherback turtle was 1,908 pounds and 8 feet, 4 inches long.

- giant tortoises are the longest living animals on earth? They grow to 600 pounds and live for 200 years.

- flying fish can cover the length of three football fields when they're airborne?

- the most deadly fish in the sea is the scorpion fish? It lives in the shallow waters and tidal pools of the Indian and Pacific Oceans. It's 2–3 feet long with eighteen venomous spines on its back. Stepping on just one spine can cause death in a few hours.

- the most poisonous of all sea creatures is the sea wasp? It's a small jellyfish found mostly off Australian beaches. Its venom can kill a person within thirty seconds of touching one if its tentacles.

Grab it by the dorsal fin and tail and pull. Once it's on board you have to kill it. It will die out of water eventually, but in the meantime, it will thrash around and can cause a lot of damage. You'll use all the energy you get from eating it repairing your raft. Surviving at sea means constantly weighing pros and cons. What you gain in one way may cause you problems in another way. You'll develop good decision-making skills while you're at sea.

Gourmet Cooking—Or How To Make Dinner in a Life raft

Now that you've got your fish, take it right to the kitchen. What kitchen? you ask. That's the point. You don't have a stove or a refrigerator at your disposal. Fish spoils quickly so you have to prepare it right away. Take out your knife and cut out the fish's gills and the large blood vessels next to its backbone. Now cut the head off. Throw these parts as far from the raft as you can and sponge up any blood that's in the raft. You don't want to attract sharks. (See the sidebar on sharks to find out just how easy it is to attract them.)

Gut any fish that's more than four inches long. That means cut open the belly and scrape out the intestines. Now scale or skin the fish. It's ready to eat raw, and will probably be very tasty. Many cultures eat fish raw all the time and even consider it a delicacy. What you can't eat in one sitting or have decided to ration can be dried for another day. Or, if you have a surplus of fresh fish but are too full to eat it, chew it to get the juice from the flesh. Chew a piece up very small, suck out the juice and swallow. Then spit out the pulp. Do this as long as you're thirsty and have enough fish.

Bon Appétit—With a Few Exceptions

As the saying goes, there are plenty of fish in the sea. But that doesn't mean you want to eat them all. Some are poisonous. But before you cough up your supper, remember that most fish in the open sea are *not* poisonous. Poisonous fish are found closer to shore. Here are some tips for recognizing poisonous fish and fish that are spoiled.

- Poisonous fish may have bristles or spines instead of true scales.
- Some poisonous fish puff up when disturbed.
- Poisonous fish are not usually found in the open sea.
- Spoiled fish have a peculiar odor. Do not eat.
- Spoiled fish may have reddish or pink gills. Do not eat.
- Spoiled fish may have slimy instead of wet bodies. The meat may also appear very gray. Do not eat.
- Spoiled fish may have a sharp or peppery taste. Do not eat.

What will happen if you do eat spoiled fish? You'll get stomach cramps and diarrhea, you'll vomit and may itch a lot. In short, you'll be sick and uncomfortable. Get the spoiled fish out of your system right away. To do this, drink some sea water and force yourself to throw up.

Beware of the red tide

The red tide is not really a tide and it's not always red. When there has been a red tide, the water will usually look brown, red, or even violet. But it may not discolor at all. A red tide occurs when *dinoflaggellates* have a population explosion. Dinoflaggellates are a kind of plankton. During very sunny, warm periods when the water currents and salt level are just right, these planktons really flourish. There are so many that they change the color of the water. Not all red tides kill fish, but some do. When there's a red tide, some of the plankton secrete poisons that kill the fish. Because there are so many dinoflaggellates, the water is robbed of its oxygen supply. The fish suffocate.

Even if the water color appears normal, don't eat fish you find dead. It may have been killed by a red tide and may pass on a poison to you. Watch out for shellfish during a red tide. They can absorb the poisons without dying. You can eat a healthy shellfish and get pretty sick. Red tides can last anywhere from a few hours to a few months. But usually they occur closer to shore.

The good news is that fish out on the open sea are usually healthy and safe to eat. So eat hearty and enjoy your catch! But even when you're sitting back enjoying a fish feast, keep on the lookout. Remember your objectives—to stay alive, healthy, and safe, *while you try to get rescued.*

Chapter 8

Navigating and Getting Rescued

Just because you're stranded at sea doesn't mean you're lost. It may be that you or someone else on board knows exactly where you are. You're just stuck there, that's all. So should you try to navigate?

Some sailors say it doesn't make sense to navigate unless you see the shore. Most boats are picked up within seven days. You can't get very far in a raft in seven days. Staying on your established course may make you easier to find once the U.S. Coastguard has your float plan.

But in some cases, navigating will make sense. It did for Steve Callahan, author of *Adrift: Seventy-Six Days Lost at Sea*. He was 450 miles from the nearest land when his boat was struck. He was outside of any regular shipping or boating routes, so his chances of being found were poor. A few weeks could pass before anyone even began searching for him.

Like most ocean sailors, he knew how to read *longitude* and *latitude*. These are the north-south and east-west lines on the globe. They're divisions made on paper as a system for pinpointing exact locations on the earth. Navigators read these maps to determine where they are, especially in vast open areas like the sea and air. Latitude and longitude are measured in degrees. For example, Buenos Aires, Argentina is thirty-five degrees south latitude and sixty degrees west longitude. If you know what direction you're headed in and how fast you're traveling, you can chart your progress on longitude and latitude maps. When you're talking to a another ship on the radio, this information can really speed up your rescue. Steve Callahan knew where the nearest shipping lanes were so he navigated toward them. Eventually, he was picked up by a fishing boat from Guadeloupe.

Which Way Am I Going?

Your compass will tell you which direction you're headed. Your knowledge of geography and the route you were following will tell you where the nearest land is. If you have oars or paddles, use them to help steer.

Your main source of power is the wind and the current. However, they may not be going in the same direction. The wind may be blowing from the south while the current is pulling you east. Which way do you go?

If the current is going where you are, take advantage of it. The lower your raft is, and the lower you ride in it, the greater the effect of the current. Sit down as low as you can. Put out your sea anchor as well.

Now if the current is moving the wrong way, but

the wind is blowing right where you want to go, the technique changes. Sit up as straight and high as you can. That way, you offer some wind resistance and act as a human sail. In fact, if you have the materials to make a sail, rig one up.

You can even measure how fast you're going. If you know how many miles to shore, you can estimate your day of arrival. That will help you ration your supplies and keep up your spirits. Information lessens the fear of the unknown.

Use a manageable piece of rope as a standard of measure. Cut it into a length of about 3 feet—a yard. Then you can measure how many rope lengths it is from say, one end of the raft to the other. Let's say it's four lengths or four yards. Now wait until you spot some seaweed in the water. When the front end of the raft reaches the seaweed, start timing. See how long it takes for the back end to arrive at the same point, the seaweed. Maybe it took thirty seconds. So, it takes half of a minute to go 4 yards. That's one minute to go 8 yards. So how far can you get in an hour? That's right—eight times sixty minutes or 480 yards. There are 2,037 yards in a nautical mile or 1,760 yards in a statute mile. Either way you look at it, you can travel roughly a quarter of a mile in an hour. That's about six miles a day. (Did you ever think those word and number problems you mastered in school would come in so handy?) Now that you know your speed, and about how far your destination is, you know how long it will take to get there.

It's possible that your compass got lost or damaged when your boat capsized. If you have a watch, you can use it as a substitute. You can experiment with this on land, too. Wait until twelve o'clock noon. Then hold your watch up horizontally so that both hands are pointing toward the sun. The hands of the watch are now pointing true south. The six points north, the nine points east, and the three points west. If you want to check your direction, but it's before or after noon, you can still determine your course. Point the hour hand to the sun. South lies midway between the twelve noon and the hour hand. So, if it's eight o'clock, the hour ten points south. If it's sunny out, put this book down, grab your watch, and go outside. Try it out and amaze your friends.

Famous Ships

By the time you reach sixth grade, most of you will have heard of the *Mayflower*. It's the ship that brought the first load of pilgrims to America. There are many other famous ships that are part of turning points in history—or, that are connected with some good stories. Here are just a few.

Acushnet—Writer Herman Melville took his first whaling voyage on this 1841, 359-ton whaler. He based his famous book, *Moby Dick,* on his experiences on this boat. (See "Sea Books and Movies.")

America—This is the famous yacht that the

America's cup is named for. She was built in 1851 and owned by a group of wealthy members of the New York Yacht Club. The Royal Yacht Club of England invited her to race around the Isle of Wight and she aced the race. The cup was named for her, and the U.S. held the cup until 1983.

April Fool—the tiniest sailboat ever to cross the Atlantic. This 5-foot, 11-inch boat sailed the 4,600 miles between Casablanca, Morocco and Del Ray, Florida in 1968. She took 84 days at an average speed of 2.7 knots.

Beagle—There have been many scientific voyages, but the most important took place on this 1831 ship. Charles Darwin traveled on this ten-gun brig gathering information that led to his theory of evolution.

Bounty—This 1789 ship was the setting for the most famous mutiny of all time. The crew became more and more upset by the unkind treatment of Captain Bligh. (See "Sea Books and Movies.")

British Red Rock—was the world's slowest ship. She took 112 days to travel the 950-mile passage across the Coral Sea in 1899. That's about 8 miles a day or about ⅓ mph. You could walk faster!

Constellation—Built in 1799, this was the first U.S. Navy warship.

Kon-Tiki—The most famous raft in history built in 1947. (See "Sea Books and Movies.")

Lusitania—The sinking of this 1915 ship led to World War I.

Potemkin—Another famous mutiny took place on this 1905 ship that was part of the beginning of the Russian Revolution.

Robert E. Lee—This 1870 Mississippi River steamer has been the subject of many stories and songs. She won an historic race up the Mississippi against the *Natchez*.

Titanic—The most famous ship disaster of all time involved this 1912 passenger boat. It was *supposed* to be an unsinkable ship.

United States—was the fastest ocean liner. On her maiden voyage in 1952, she averaged about 41 miles an hour. She crossed 2,949 nautical miles in about 3½ days. *United States* steamed the longest distance covered by a ship in one day—868 nautical miles.

Signs of Land

Even if you don't know which direction land is, you can look for signs of it. If you see a sign of land, navigate towards it. These signs are written in the sky, the air, and the sea.

Signs of Land in the Sky

- One nice, puffy cumulus cloud in a clear sky, or in a sky where all the other clouds are moving. The cumulus cloud is hovering right over or just downwind from an island.

- A line of cumulus clouds. These hang over a coastline.

- A greenish-blue tint to the sky or on the bottom of a cloud. That's caused by the reflection of the shallow water of a lagoon or a reef.

- A glare in the sky at night may be the lights of a city.

Signs of Land in the Air

- Watch the flight of birds. At dawn they fly from land to a feeding area. At dusk they fly from a feeding area back to land.

- Insects and odors travel on the wind from land. Especially after a rain, you may smell earth and vegetation. Travel in the direction the wind is coming from. That's where those smells, or bugs, originate.

- Listen well. Sounds can really travel over water. You'll hear the sound of the surf and breakers before you see it.

- Feel the air around you. The morning breezes blow in the opposite direction of the evening breezes. Air flows *from* the land at midnight until early morning. Then the breezes blow *toward* the land from the hours before noon into the evening. These breezes can be felt up to 15–20 miles from the coast.

Signs of Land in the Sea

- Muddy water with a sweet taste means river water. Rivers mean land. Some rivers flow out to sea for many miles, so the land may be out of sight.

- There are more fish near land than in the open sea. Sea lions and seals mean land is nearby.

- Driftwood and a lot of vegetation are carried off-shore by currents. If you see some driftwood floating in the water, that's a sign of land.

Getting Rescued

In order to get rescued someone has to spot you. It's harder than you might think to see a small raft drifting among the waves. You have to make yourself as obvious as possible. Yet, your signaling supplies are limited. Don't waste them. Always wait until a ship or an aircraft is in sight before you use your distress signals. But in the meantime, it can't hurt to use an ancient method. Put a letter stating the date, your approximate position, and your physical condition in a plastic bag. Tape the bag to a piece of Styrofoam and float it out into the water. It will be carried by wind and current faster than you will. Perhaps another boat will find it. Repeat your message for help every few days. It will give you hope, and you never know where help will come from.

Daytime Signaling

Orange smoke is very visible from a distance during the day. Commercial visual distress signals, the ones you buy in supply stores, give off about two minutes worth of orange smoke. Two minutes may seem like a lifetime while you stand there holding your smoke device waiting for the boat in the distance to start coming your way. But as you know when you're out riding your bike, two minutes isn't very long. So I'll say it once more—don't waste the smoke. Only use it when a ship is in sight or an aircraft can be heard. The day should be clear and not too windy. In winds over ten knots, the smoke will be dispersed and won't be of any use. Orange flares are standard equipment in boating emergency kits.

Distress flags are made in bright orange with a black circle and square on it. This design really catches the eye in bright sunlight. Wave it from a paddle or a mast. It's very effective.

Night Signals

At night, put away the orange and take out the red. Red is the color for night. There's an effective signaling device called a *red meteor* or *star*. This is something like mini-fireworks. It shoots up and comes down quickly. The light is bright but short-lived. Only fire it when you can see the lights of another boat.

You can send out a powerful SOS with a *distress signal lantern*. Flash this international distress signal of three dots, three dashes, three dots. In light language that translates to three short flashes, three long flashes, and three short flashes again. Flash slowly sending the full SOS about four to six times a minute. A flashlight can be used to flash the same signal, but it has very limited power. It would be difficult to alert a boat more than one mile away.

Night and Day

Red parachute flares will work night or day. They go up and come down slowly, which is an advantage. They last longer and they're very bright, so, you have time and power on your side. Carry at least three red parachute flares if you chose this distress signal. *Red hand-held flares* also have good visibility. Take some safety precautions when using these or the *orange daytime flares*. Hold the flare at arm's length away from your body, at about a forty-five-degree angle. Keep a firm grip. Point the flare downwind so that hot residue doesn't blow toward you and burn you.

Sea markers are used to attract aircraft. This device is a flourescent orange powder. When it's released in the sea, it makes a light green flourescent cast. Just a little packet of this stuff spreads out about 150 feet. In calm weather the effect will last about an hour. In rough seas, however, it's not very effective. It just streaks the water and the color is lost among the waves. But in the best conditions, a sea marker can be spotted from five miles away when an aircraft is one thousand feet up. It can be seen for seven miles if the aircraft is at 2,000 feet. Use your sea marker only when you can see or hear a plane, and not in heavy fog.

① Aiming mirror with stationary object

② Aiming mirror when angle between the sun and help exceeds 180°

How to hold your signal mirror if 1) your potential rescuer is not moving or 2) the sun is behind you and the plane is in front of you.

A *signal mirror* is a popular device on land or at sea. It's a small mirror with a little hole in it. Here's how to use it. First catch the sun's reflection on the mirror. Reflect the light from the mirror onto your hand. Slowly bring the mirror up to your eye. Look through the hole. You can see a bright spot of light. Aim that light toward the sight or sound of an aircraft. Hold the flash in place until the plane starts coming your way. Once the pilot starts coming toward you, take the flash away, as the light can be blinding. Just give occasional signals to guide the plane toward you. If you practice with your signal mirror at home, *don't aim it at a passing aircraft.* If the aircraft is low enough, you may temporarily blind or confuse the pilot. Just use the roof of your house or apartment building as a target.

If you don't have a signal mirror in your emergency kit, any shiny object will do. Polish a metal cup or a belt buckle. Whatever casts a reflection will work.

Uh-Oh, We Ran Out

What do you do if you run out of commercial distress signals and you still haven't been rescued? You do what you've been doing all along. You improvise. Use anything you have to create a signal. Tie together bright clothing and shiny objects that may catch the sunlight. Wave them or tie them to a paddle. Steve Callahan made a kite by cutting a swatch of his reflective space blanket and fastening it to a frame. In fact, as he created the signal, it occurred to him that a real kite would be a good piece of emergency equipment. They usually come in bright colors and can soar thousands of feet high. You might want to include one in your kit.

"Mayday, Mayday, Mayday"

A radio is one of the most important pieces of emergency equipment. Ship radios are designed to be waterproof, so if you didn't lose yours in the wreck, it should still work. Radio transmissions are internationally recognized as distress signals. In fact, for three minutes twice every hour there are silence periods at sea. That means that no transmissions except distress and safety signals can be broadcasted. The airwaves are free for those who need help.

The Coast Guard has established basic procedures for proper distress communications. If you follow them your chances of rescue are greater.

1) Check to be sure your radio is on. This may sound pretty basic, but it's natural to be a little confused and forgetful.

2) Tune into the distress frequency. It's Channel 16 for FM, 2 MHz or 2182 kHz for Radiotelephone, and Channel 9 for Citizens Band.

3) Press the microphone button. Say, "Mayday, mayday, mayday." Why "mayday"? Mayday is a distress call for ships and aircraft. A message preceded by the mayday signal gets top priority. The words probably come from the French *m'aidez*, which means "help me." It's pronounced mayday.

4) Clearly identify yourself. Say your boat's name, (the one that was destroyed) three times: "This is the *Pink Dolphin,* the *Pink Dolphin,* the *Pink Dolphin.*" Then give your *call sign.* Your call sign is a number assigned to your radio. You get it by registering the radio with the Federal Communications Commission (FCC). This number helps identify you. A call sign sounds something like this: Whiskey, *X*-ray, *November 7763.* The letters *WXN* are part of the call sign. The words

whiskey, x-ray, and November are their pho-
netic equivalents. That means they're the FCC-
designated words for clarifying which letter you
said. It's important that people understand your
speech clearly so there's no confusion about
where the call is coming from.

5) Give your position. Give as much information
about where you are as you can. Site any land-
marks. Hopefully, the captain of your crew can
determine approximate longitude and latitude.

6) Now say what's wrong. Get right to the point.
You've been adrift in a life raft for four days.
Your boat was rammed by a whale.

7) Say what kind of help you need.

8) Say how many people are on the raft. If anyone
is sick or injured, describe their condition.

9) Give the condition of your raft. If you've just had
your shipwreck and are still on the boat, mention how long you think she has until you'll have
to abandon ship.

10) Describe the boat or raft. Tell what type it is,
what color, and the size.

11) Tell which channel you'll be listening on for reply. If you're listening on a different frequency
than the one they respond on, you could lose your
opportunity for help.

12) Here's how you end the message. "This is the
Pink Dolphin, Whiskey, X-ray, November 7763.
Over."

13) Wait for an answer. If you don't get one, give
the message again. If there's still no reply, repeat the message on another frequency or
channel.

When the Coast Guard gets your transmission, they may ask a lot of questions. The questions may seem irrelevant to you, but the information will help a rescue team serve you better. Meanwhile, as you answer questions, help is on the way. It won't be long before you're back on the soccer field kicking that winning goal.

Chapter 9

First Aid at Sea

Part of being safe at sea is knowing what to avoid. Serious health problems can usually be prevented. First, you have to know what they are. While you're afloat, the greatest dangers are exposure to the cold and wind and dehydration.

Dehydration

What it is: When you're dehydrated it basically means you need water. You've lost body fluids, and they haven't been replaced. There are different degrees of dehydration. Here's how you can tell if it's getting serious.

Signs: The best way to tell if you're becoming dehydrated is by checking your urine. It's odd, but you can't rely on your feelings of thirst. Thirst sensations lag behind the body's need for water. You should be urinating at least three times a day. Your urine should be light-colored. When your urine becomes dark in color, dehydration has become serious. You may feel dizzy, have a headache, and have trouble breathing. You may feel and act quite irritable.

What to do: At the first signs of dehydration, drink as much fresh water as you can without seriously depleting the supply. Never drink seawater or urine. You'll use up more body water flushing out the salts in both of these fluids than you'll get by drinking them. Keep shaded and rest.

Hypothermia

What it is: Hypothermia is a dangerous cooling of the inner core of the body. It occurs when you're immersed in water cooler than your body temperature for long periods. Even though you're on a raft, if your clothing is wet and it's cold out, you're at risk for hypothermia.

Signs: When the body temperature has dropped below 95 degrees, a person may become sluggish. The person's coordination is poor and so is his/her judgement. At its worst, hypothermia can result in unconsciousness and eventually death.

What to do: As long as you're out of the water, you can avoid fatal hypothermia, but you or someone in your group can get dangerously chilled. If that happens, put modesty and the usual conventions aside. Gently remove the wet clothing. Wrap the naked, chilled person in a warm sleeping bag or blanket with another warm, naked person. This is very important. The chilled person should not be wrapped in a blanket alone. He or she needs the warm contact with another body. If you have some honey or sugar, feed some to the victim.

Don't rub frozen body areas and *don't* give the victim anything to drink. Incorrect treatment of hypothermia can lead to a condition called *afterdrop*.

This occurs when the victim has been rewarmed the wrong way. Rubbing the extremities causes cold blood from the arms and legs to return to the core of the body. The cold blood may bring the body temperature down to a fatal level. It's important to warm the head, sides, neck, and groin first. This is best done by nude body-to-body contact.

You can avoid a serious chill at sea by putting up a wind shelter. Keep your limbs tucked in close to your body like a bird at rest. Huddle together with your fellow sailors. Wiggle your toes, fingers, nose, and ears to prevent frostbite. Put your hands between your thighs or under your armpits for a quick warm-up.

Immersion Foot

What it is: Immersion foot is a condition that results from your feet being immersed in the cold, wet, crampy conditions that can occur in open lifeboats. Circulation in the feet becomes very poor.

Signs: The feet swell, become numb, and turn purplish or very pale. They feel waxy.

What to do: Prevent it. Keep your feet as dry as you can. Carry extra socks in a plastic bag in your survival kit. If you don't have extra dry socks, take off your wet ones and wrap your feet in any cloth that's dry. Then put the wet socks against your skin to dry them. Keep the boat well bailed. Keep wiggling your toes and flexing your ankles for improved circulation. Try to put your feet up for a few minutes out of every hour. If you start to show signs of immersion foot, remove your socks and put your feet between someone's thighs or under his arms. Don't rub your feet. As in hypothermia, just warm them slowly through contact with a heat source, like another person.

Saltwater Sores

What they are: Saltwater sores are breaks in the skin that occur when you've been exposed to saltwater for an extended period of time. Basically, the skin is soaked through with seawater. These sores or boils can be very painful.

Signs: Redness, scabs, and pus form around ulcers in the skin.

What to do: Flush the sores with fresh water if possible. Only use water to wash them if your supply is plentiful. The boils are uncomfortable, but they can be tolerated better than dehydration. Save your water for drinking if there's any doubt that you'll have enough to last you until you're rescued.

Don't open or squeeze the boils. Dry the sores well, apply an antiseptic, and cover them with bandages if possible.

Raft Health Hazards

What they are. Because of the cramped and crowded conditions on a life raft, your body has a lot to put up with. Cramps, constipation, fainting, sores, blisters, and calluses are all part of the survival picture. Let's take these minor but annoying ailments one at a time.

Cramps. When you're confined in a small craft, your muscles may cramp up. Flex your muscles and bend your joints often. Give each other massages unless you're experiencing frostbite or hypothermia (see explanation in this chapter).

Constipation. Lack of exercise and water can lead to constipation. One sailor adrift at sea went thirty-five days without a bowel movement. Long periods between bowel movements is common in sea survival. Actually, there are some advantages to this. There's not a lot of unnecessary residue in the often scanty rations you get at sea. In other words, there's not much waste for your body to eliminate. Passing wastes requires water, so less frequent bowel movements means less use of body fluid. This doesn't mean that it's desirable to be constipated, but it's not something to worry about.

Fainting. We haven't talked much about sleep while you're adrift. However, you may have guessed that it's not exactly a case of lights out and sweet dreams. Your sleeping quarters are cramped. You probably have some duties as lookout. After all, a boat could pass at any time and you don't want to sleep through an opportunity to be rescued. Needless to say, you're not your usual energetic self. Sudden movements may cause light-headedness and giddiness. You may even faint. Just move slowly and rest with your head between your knees.

Blisters and Calluses. Blisters, calluses, and other skin irritations develop from a combination of friction and pressure. Handling ropes, sitting on hard surfaces for long periods, and exposure to sun and cold are inevitable conditions. Try to keep any irritated area dry, clean, and covered. Change position often and sit on something soft if possible, like a cushion or a roll of clothes.

Here Comes the Sun

What that means: A sunny day has advantages and disadvantages. It usually means that you'll be warm and dry, but it may mean a short water supply. And it definitely means:

Sunburn

Signs: Your skin is warm to the touch. When you press on it with your finger, the indentation turns white for a second and then back to pink. In a while, it feels hot, dry, and painful.

What to do: Avoid sunburn by keeping your body covered. Wear a hat or tie a handkerchief over your head. Roll down your sleeves and pull up your collar. Wear sunglasses to protect your eyes from the direct ultra-violet rays of the sun, or from rays reflected off the water. If you have no glasses, cut eye slits in a bandana and wrap the bandana around your head. If you do get burned, apply cream from your first aid kit and cover the area.

Heat or Sun Stroke

What it is: It's the opposite of hypothermia and occurs when the body temperature is way too high.

Signs: Very hot, dry skin. Also weakness, dizziness, nausea, and rapid breathing. The pulse is strong and fast.

What to do: First, you have to lower the victim's body temperature. This should be done quickly.

Shade the victim and cover him or her with cold, wet cloths. Rub his/her arms and legs toward the heart to increase blood flow. Replace the wet cloths with cold ones every ten minutes or so.

Fish Bites and Stings

What they are: Some fish have spikes or spines. Some have a powerful bite. You may have some mini-battles with your catch with wounds to show for it.
Signs: It will be obvious.
What to do: Apply ointment and cover the wound with a bandage. Don't rub it.
Note: In all your wild fishing adventures, you may end up hooking yourself. If a fishhook gets embedded in your finger, press down on the stem of the hook, which is called the *shank*. Keep pushing the shank in until the barbed end pushes out through the skin. It may make the process easier if you make a small cut in your skin at the point where the hook is trying to come out. Now cut off the barbed end of the hook with pliers and slide out the remaining shaft. Wash the wound with soap and bandage it.

Seasickness

What it is: Seasickness is caused by stimulation to the non-hearing sense organs of the inner ear. The motion of the boat is the stimulus that causes the inner ear to send a certain pattern of nerve impulses to the brain. Fatigue can make you more prone to seasickness, but it has nothing to do with your attitude. The best of sailors get it, especially in a small craft that's low in the water, like your raft.

Symptoms: Pale skin, cold sweats, nausea, and vomiting.

What to do: Take seasickness pills if you have them. In a couple of days your body is likely to adjust to the raft conditions and the discomfort will pass. In the meantime, lie down and rest. Don't eat until the nausea is gone. Wash the victim and the raft to remove all vomit. The sight and odor of it is contagious and can attract sharks.

Some survivors recommend using a spot on the horizon as a focal point. This trick, called spotting, is what ballet dancers use when they do all those rapid spins. Dancers choose one fixed point in the room to "spot" every time they do a full turn. This keeps the dancer from getting dizzy. So keep staring ahead at a steady point on the horizon and the nausea may subside.

Others say swimming alongside the raft for short periods helps seasickness. However, you must be very careful if you do this. The water and air must be warm, and the area free of sharks.

A *seasick strap* is a new remedy that research has proven effective. The strap presses on an acupuncture pressure point near the wrist. Acupuncture is an ancient Chinese system of medicine that is used around the world. Acupuncturists believe that different points on the body correspond to other parts inside the body. Pressure is put on certain points to relieve pain or disease.

The seasick strap is a four-inch piece of elastic about two-thirds of an inch wide. It opens and closes with Velcro. In the center of the strap is a plastic button. The button is worn against the acupuncture point on the skin and applies constant pressure. According to Dr. Daniel Shu Jen Choy, an internist affiliated with Columbia Presbyterian Hospital in Manhattan, the acupuncture pressure point is "on the surface of the forearm, three finger widths above the crease of the wrist and in the center, between the two flex tendons." Experiments show that the strap works in 70 percent of the cases of seasickness tested.

Your Sea First Aid Kit

Inside your waterproof survival kit should be a waterproof first aid kit. All the survival and first aid items should have their own instructions. You should already be familiar with the items and know how to use them. Here's what you should have inside the first aid kit.

- several packs of seasick tablets and two seasick straps
- bandaids, guaze bandages, and tape
- needles, safety and straight pins, a small scissors and tweezers
- aspirin
- protective sunscreen, sunburn lotion and first aid cream.
- antiseptic lotion for cleaning cuts

And now, back to the Baileys.

Chapter 10

The Rescue

When we left the Baileys, they were 117 days adrift. Maralyn heard a ship in the distance—the eighth one since their ordeal began on March 4, 1973. It was June 30. With no commercial or homemade distress signals left, there was nothing to do but wave their clothes and shout for help. Maurice and Maralyn waved madly, but when the ship passed, Maurice gave up hope.

Always the optimist, Maralyn continued to wave and call. Maurice looked at her pitifully. He knew Maralyn would not stop trying until the ship had completely disappeared. She shouted from the depths of her belly, and then their miracle occurred. The ship started coming back! The Baileys could hardly believe their eyes. They put their clothes on with the kind of wild energy that only comes after total despair. They joyously let the two captive turtles in the dinghy go free and wished them well.

The Korean fishing boat came up alongside the small raft that had supported the Baileys for almost four months. The crew sent down ropes to haul the raft up to their boat, the *Weolmi 36*. The *Weolmi* was a tuna fishing boat on its way home to South Korea after thirty months of fishing in the Atlantic.

Maralyn tried to stand and found that she couldn't. After four months of sitting, her legs were too weak to hold her up. The crew lifted her onto the *Weolmi*. The ship's cook was ready with hot, steaming milk. The Baileys were surrounded by smiling faces. "We've made it," sighed Maurice. "Now for *Auralyn II*—and Patagonia!" said Maralyn.

At that moment, the Baileys had no idea that they would be world news. They spent the next two weeks on the Korean boat who radioed the mainland about this remarkable couple. The crew was very kind to the Baileys. They gave Maurice and Maralyn gifts of clothing, soaps, cosmetics and chocolates that they had intended for their own families. The fishermen even gave the Baileys their personal supplies of tuna. The Korean boat was an ideal place for the couple to renew human contact. The Baileys grew stronger in this atmosphere of generosity and love.

On Friday, July 13, the *Weolmi 36* arrived on Oahu, a Hawaiian island. There was a huge reception for them. They were guests of the Sheraton Waikiki where they received complete medical work-ups. The crew of the *Weolmi* waited for the Baileys who hoped to go with the fishermen to South Korea. But Maralyn and Maurice required medical care and supplies that the fishing boat couldn't provide. So they said a sad good-bye to their rescuers and new friends.

"Annyoughi Kesipsiyo, Ch'ukpok hapnida!" they called, which means good-bye and good luck in Korean. Maralyn and Maurice Bailey promised to visit the crew of the *Weolmi 36* on their next voyage—on the *Auralyn II!*

114

Sea Books and Movies

You can travel out to sea in the pages of a book or the images on a screen. Try one of these as your ticket to adventure.

Books to Read Alone or Aloud with Your Family

Kon-Tiki, by Thor Heyerdahl

Moby Dick, by Herman Melville

Robinson Crusoe, by Daniel Defoe

The Old Man and the Sea, by Ernest Hemingway

The Odyssey, by Homer

Movies

Some of these films are old black and white movies, but don't let that discourage you from watching them. The acting is very good and the stories are exciting. They've thrilled viewers for many years. Because some of the movies were made fifty years ago, they may portray characters in a stereotypical way. Men are the heroes and women are in distress. White-skinned people are powerful and people of color are servants. Remember to look beyond this. You can see through sexism and racism and still find a good story. Watch with a critical eye—and enjoy!

Black Stallion, 1979 with Kelly Reno and Mickey Rooney. This dramatic story of a boy and a wild horse begins on a ship.

Boy on a Dolphin, 1957 with Alan Ladd and Sophia Loren. A sunken treasure sea adventure.

Captain Blood, 1935 with Errol Flynn. A pirate-on-the-high-seas adventure.

Captains Courageous, 1937 with Spencer Tracy and Freddie Bartholomew. Rudyard Kipling's story of a Portuguese fisherman who rescues a boy who fell off an ocean liner.

China Seas, 1935 with Clark Gable and Jean Harlow. Passengers on a boat from Hong Kong to Singapore encounter storms and pirates.

Lifeboat, 1944 with Tallulah Bankhead. Survivors of a passenger ship sunk by a German submarine in WWII are adrift at sea.

Moby Dick, 1956 with Gregory Peck and Richard Basehart. Captain Ahab struggles to land a fierce white whale.

Mutiny on the Bounty, 1935 with Charles Laughton and Clark Gable. The crew is provoked to mutiny by the cruel Captain Bligh.

Old Man and the Sea, 1958 with Spencer Tracy. An old man braves the stormy sea trying to catch a big fish.

Poseidon Adventure, 1972 with Gene Hackman and Ernest Borgnine. Passengers trapped in a capsized luxury liner try to survive.

The Sea Gypsies, 1978 with Robert Logan. This family adventure is about a man and his daughters marooned on the Alaskan coast.

Sinbad the Sailor, 1947 with Douglas Fairbanks, Jr. and Maureen O'Hara. A high seas adventure with lost treasure.

Swiss Family Robinson, 1960 with John Mills and Dorothy McGuire. This is the Disney version of the Johann Wyss classic story of a shipwrecked family.

20,000 Leagues Under the Sea, 1954 with Kirk Douglas and James Mason. Walt Disney production of Jules Verne's story of life on a futuristic submarine.

Bibliography

Bailey, Maurice and Maralyn. *Staying Alive*. New York: David McKay Co., Inc., 1974.

Callahan, Steven. *Adrift: 76 Days Lost at Sea*. New York: Ballantine Books, 1986.

Chapman, Charles F. *Piloting Seamanship and Small Boat Handling*. New York: The Hearst Corporation, 1967.

Engel, Leonard. *The Sea*. New York: Time-Life, Inc., 1983.

Freuchen, Peter. *Book of the Seven Seas*. New York: Julian Messner, Inc., 1957.

Groves, Don. *The Oceans: A Book of Questions and Answers*. New York: John Wiley & Sons, 1989.

Hendrickson, Robert. *The Ocean Almanac*. New York: Doubleday & Co., 1984.

Lee, E.C.B. and Kenneth. *Safety and Survival at Sea*. New York: W.W. Norton & Co., 1980.

Robertson, Dougal. *Survive the Savage Seas*. New York: Praeger Publishers, 1973.

Search and Rescue Survival Training. Washington, D.C.: Department of the Air Force, 1985.

Shepard, Francis P. *The Earth Beneath the Sea*. Baltimore: Johns Hopkins Press, 1967.

Survival. Washington, D.C.: Department of the Army, 1986.